POWER
TO THE
SCHOOLS

SUCESSFUL SCHOOLS
Guidebooks to Effective Educational Leadership
Fenwick W. English, Series Editor

POWER TO THE SCHOOLS

School
Leader's
Guidebook to
Restructuring

William J. Bailey

CORWIN PRESS, INC.
A Sage Publications Company
Newbury Park, California

Copyright © 1992 by Corwin Press, Inc.

For information address:

Corwin Press
A Sage Publications Company
2455 Teller Road
Newbury Park, California 91320

SAGE Publications Ltd.
6 Bonhill Street
London EC2A 4PU
United Kingdom

SAGE Publications India Pvt. Ltd.
M-32 Market
Greater Kailash I
New Delhi 110 048 India

Printed in the United States of America

Library of Congress Cataloging-in-Publication Data

Bailey, William J. 1929–
    Power to the Schools : school leader's guidebook to restructuring
/ William J. Bailey.
      p.   cm. — (Successful schools ; v. 8)
    Includes bibliographical references.
    ISBN 0–8039–6017–4
    1. School management and organization—United States.
2. Educational change—United States. I. Title. II. Series.
LB2805.B18   1992
371.2'00973—dc20   92-335
                                           CIP

92 93 94 95 10 9 8 7 6 5 4 3 2 1

Corwin Press Production Editor: Tara S. Mead

Contents

NOTES

Foreword

The "in" word these days in American education is *restructuring*. As the case with so many terms before it, such as team teaching, career ladders, merit pay, and accountability, it has come to take on meanings that are contradictory and confusing.

Bill Bailey offers a book on the topic that is enormously practical and applicable. Bailey begins with the central office, the most visible *obstacle* to restructuring. This tactic is born of the observation that simply restructuring schools without considering the actual system in which they function is an exercise in futility. Just as schools make up the school system, so does the system, as represented in the central office, shape the schools. So both must be *restructured*.

Bailey recognizes both the enormously complicated task of restructuring and the "empowerment" issue associated with it. He develops the topics of awareness and readiness and provides a checklist for the school administrator to follow to ensure that teachers are prepared for the kinds of changes true restructuring requires. The critical notion of governance, the actual avenue for altering administrative power, is explored and detailed as well.

Bailey is a former secondary school principal turned professor, who deeply believes schools can be more democratic and effective places in which teachers can live, interact, and teach, and students can interact and learn. His practical administrative experience and his idealism blend together nicely in this straightforward narrative of the changes necessary if American schools are to remain viable as effective social mechanisms, helping to perpetuate democracy and improve our way of life.

Professor Bailey was instrumental in establishing a very successful and innovative doctoral program for school administrators at the University of Delaware. He currently has accepted the same challenge at Appalachian State University in Boone, North Carolina. I wouldn't be surprised if some of the readers of this book end up in his classes in beautiful Boone to learn more from this thoughtful practitioner-professor. If that should occur, be prepared for a wonderful and thoughtful dialogue that this book only initiates.

FENWICK W. ENGLISH
Univeristy of Kentucky

Preface

There is a crisis in education lurking just outside your office door! At least, if administrators and school board members listen to the critics of public education, one would believe a crisis was imminent. Even if educational leaders don't believe all of the "doomsday" messages, we all would like to have better schools.

Problem: How do public schools get better?
Solution: They constantly adapt to whatever changes are necessary to enable them to be effective—given the context in which they exist.

Probably as an educational leader, you admit that some changes are called for; but do you realize that the typical, traditional public school district is not structured to adapt to serious change? With all of the pressures to reform education, the fact is that we are dealing with an organizational structure that is the antithesis of change. Public schools have evolved in such a way that the basic organizational structure, operational practices, and normative behavior resist anything that's threatening to the organization. Public school leaders tend to resist anything new except a slow, evolutionary, and gradual change. In other words, if school districts make any significant change, it happens so slowly that the change is not noticeable. Therefore changes that occur are not a direct result of management strategies. *Current school districts are not adaptable.*

Meanwhile, the critics are calling for a "revolution." In the midst of these calls for revolution, educational leaders are powerless because they are driving great big, bulky school buses, when, to meet the challenges of the twenty-first century, these leaders need the power of driving a fleet of small sports cars. And these cars do not even have to be a matched fleet! They just need to be agile enough to manipulate the obstacle courses established by the call for reform.

I submit that most of the real and imagined problems besieging the public schools today are related to the basic organizational power and structure of public school districts. In fact, the larger the district, the more these problems are exaggerated. Consequently, we must change the basic structure of school district organization—in other words, *restructure*—and we must use power more effectively—in other words, *empower.*

This book, as part of the Successful Schools series, is designed to assist educational leaders in the transformation necessary to restructure and empower. Although there are no easy paths or solutions, there are some practical strategies that can be administered in such a way that puts decision makers in the management driver's seat. This book will tell you how to manage that "fleet of unmatched sports cars."

Chapter 1 is designed to acquaint you with the specific problems caused by the current structure. I have pointed to the advantages of creating a system that is more adaptable to change. It is possible to unblock your organization, and Chapter 1 starts you on this path.

Then, Chapter 2 explains the specific management techniques needed to restructure your district from a school district system to a system of schools. School site management is introduced.

In Chapter 3, I delineate the procedures for empowering faculty, basically through the deployment of work teams. When we hear the word *empowerment,* we naturally wonder whether teachers are professional enough to handle these new responsibilities. The steps to take to increase professionalism in any school staff are discussed in Chapter 4.

Because learning is what schools are about, it is important to develop means of constantly improving achievement in schools. Chapter 5 is devoted to improving student learning in a decentralized system with a special emphasis on increasing instructional time.

From two decades of research on the change process in schools, educators should be knowledgeable about change strategies. Chapter 6 reviews our knowledge base regarding the principles of change and innovation as a management behavior.

Chapter 7 deals with the problems of accountability, which are certainly on everyone's mind. Options are developed from which the administrator can choose to implement. And, finally, there is a Troubleshooting Guide for the reader to use as an index for solutions to problems encountered. These problems are predictable and the guidelines should assist leaders in having ready answers.

Although this is a problem-solving book, I realize that every situation is different. The suggestions spelled out here are sound, based on research, and guided by my personal experience as an administrator and a consultant to more than 130 different organizations. Each educational leader, however, must be a reflective practitioner and pick and choose from viable alternatives. It is my hope that the book will leave readers with enough of these alternatives so that the thoughtful change agent will be successful.

Good luck!

WILLIAM J. BAILEY
Appalachian State University

NOTES

About the Author

William J. Bailey (Ed.D.) has been active as a consultant, re-
searcher, and writer since entering higher educationas a Professor
of Educational Leadership at the University of Delaware. Prior
to the University of Delaware, he served as a teacher in both
public and independent schools, as a principal in both Michigan
and Delaware, and as an associate superintendent in Delaware.
This practical experience has enabled him to bring to practitioners such publications as *Managing Self Renewal in Secondary
Education* (Educational Technology), *Strategies for School Improvement* (Allyn & Bacon), *The Professional Growth Trilogy:
Supervision, Evaluation and Staff Development* (Independent
School Management), *School Site Management Applied* (Technomic), and a book on leadership, which is in press with Technomic. He has written more than 35 articles and book reviews,
served on the Board of Directors for ASCD and the National
Council of States, received several excellence in teaching
awards, and consulted with a variety of public and private organizations. He received his B.S. in Education and an M.A. in Educational Administration from the University of Michigan and an

Ed.D. from Michigan State University. He currently is Professor and Director of Doctoral Programs in Educational Leadership at Appalachian State University in Boone, North Carolina, and has a home in Pinehurst, North Carolina, where he enjoys playing golf.

1

Problems Facing School Structure Today

1.1 Major Problems Caused by the Structure and Systems of Power in Our Schools

John Gardner once remarked that each day we are faced with a series of great opportunities brilliantly disguised as unsolvable problems. What are the seemingly unsolvable problems of education today? Educational critics do not seem to have any difficulty in identifying these problems, but educators are quick to say "our hands are tied." Perhaps the greatest opportunities for solving problems lie in looking at the basic structure and governance system intrinsic to school districts. Consequently, this leader's notebook on restructuring is presented.

Elmore et al. (1990, p. 4) cogently submit: "A major policy question in the debate over restructured schools, to paraphrase Gertrude Stein's famous line about Oakland, California, is, 'when you get there, is there any there, there?' " When and if a school district restructures, what does it have? There will be no "there" unless the *reasons* for restructuring and/or empowering were sound, rational, and well planned. Elmore et al. (1990, p. 4) further question: "Is there enough substance behind restructuring proposals to constitute a reform agenda, and if there is, what political and practical problems does the agenda raise?" Without significant changes for substantive reasons, there is no need to restructure.

For example, it does not make any sense to restructure for the following reasons:

- The board thought it would be a good idea.
- Our test scores are low.
- The professional literature is filled with advice articles about restructuring.
- My professor at the university is in favor of it.
- I heard we could save money.
- School site management is very popular now.
- The state is encouraging it.

I believe there is one major reason to restructure. Our current school systems' organizational structures are not—I repeat, *not* —designed to accommodate change. Organizational design and the table of organization guide the school district but definitely create blocks to change. In education, there has been, and will continue to be, constant pendulum swings in ideas about proper education. Sometimes these "new ideas" reach enough momentum to be called a "reform movement"; sometimes they are referred to as "innovations"; but they keep coming. The major problem school districts have is in attempting to adopt and adapt to new trends. The typical school system structure is not designed to accommodate constant and responsive change. Bureaucracy is not working in the schools anyway—let alone changing.

The following are examples of problems experienced by most school administrators and school board members that are related to structure:

1. It is difficult to install shared authority concepts because many teachers resist (Raywid, 1990). Installing shared authority seems to move even more slowly than other changes.

2. Even if people agree to make significant changes, many persist in conducting themselves in the same way as before the "change." In other words, the change is not internalized (Raywid, 1990). As a result, otherwise cooperative faculty are actually noncomplying. After extensive time and money have been spent on staff and curriculum development, teachers still close their doors and teach the way they were taught.

3. Communication continues to be a larger and larger problem.

4. The harder you try for standardization of operational procedures, the more there are constant deviations. For example, a districtwide curriculum supervised by the director of instruction still presents problems in quality control.

5. Parents complain about unequal treatment of their children in comparison with the programs children receive in other schools within the district.

6. Distributing sparse amounts of public funds becomes increasingly difficult given budget cutbacks and slowdowns. Knowing how to distribute the funds equally is an ever-present problem.

7. There are a few principals who are not productive and attempts to change them, "build a fire under them," or to threaten them have not been particularly successful. They cannot be fired and they cannot be motivated.

8. There continue to be relationship problems between district office staff (supervisors, curriculum coordinators, and support services) and building-level administrators.

9. Teacher morale is low, and stress is high.

10. Much effort is spent on creating representative mechanisms such as councils, task forces, and committees but there is not a resulting payoff—and many voices remain unheard. Some of these "voices" eventually sabotage new programs. Negotiations are a problem because the process is still an adversarial one instead of one of problem solving (Cohee, 1991).

11. It is difficult to make the school district responsive to the external environment.
12. Principals complain that, although they are asked to be strong instructional leaders, they are given very little managerial freedom.
13. Achievement test scores are still too low.

All of the above problems identified in varying degrees by most administrators are a direct effect of the organizational design. Overbureaucratization has resulted from the general assumption that one can control loosely coupled organizations from the top down. This notion is strangling motivation and effectiveness. This top-down power does not work. School leaders must "power down."

Let's look at what structure has done to create some of these problems and then reinforce the premise that the main reason for restructuring is to establish an organization that is capable of change.

1.2 Restructuring Can Solve Problems

Let's look at each one of the sample problems in light of structure and/or governance perspectives.

A. *The Difficulty of Installing Shared Authority Concepts*

Structural point of view. What has been the past experience of the majority of teachers in most districts? Teachers have been conditioned (with the best of intentions) to take orders; that is, they know very well there is a principal who reacts to the superintendent's wishes, suggestions, and directives. The hierarchical system has been working too well. Even though teachers are told to form a committee and make the decision, they still don't believe this new order. Eventually, if the new structure establishes that all major decisions are made at the school level, teachers will begin to believe in the new system. This "unfreezing," "re-creating," and "refreezing" takes several years, however.

B. *Changes Are Not Internalized*

Structural point of view. Teachers' behaviors have been modeled from observations as a student and as a student teacher-supervisor. This process sets a rigid standard that is difficult to break. Only with concerted, daily interaction with teaching peers will those old habits be broken. The isolationist conditioning of the self-contained class (a historic structural decision) has been thorough; it has forced teachers to conduct their professional behavior with little or infrequent supervision. The old pattern goes like this: Agree to a change but go to your workstation, behind the classroom door, and teach the way you have always taught. The threat of being "noncomplying" is not as compelling as old habits. The systems of power have broken down. Change the system.

C. *Communication Problems*

Structural point of view. Have you ever witnessed a high school homeroom when the announcements are being read over the intercom? That's right, very few are paying any—or, at best, slight—attention. Why? The immediate attention from peers is a stronger pull. The message over the intercom is boring, remote, said by a faceless person, and therefore is not effective. New patterns must be made for school communication effectiveness. For example, don't have a homeroom. Have a teacher or a student government representative in a regular classroom discuss the coming events. The goal of homerooms designed to personalize the comprehensive high school has been displaced. Ironically, eliminating homeroom is now one way to personalize the high school.

Another example is when faculty receive memorandums. Teachers don't read them because their peers had nothing to do with the source. More important is listening to a fellow teacher complain about a student. If it's not worth walking down the hall to tell someone, it probably isn't worthwhile to communicate anyway.

Gore Associates, a very successful multibillion-dollar corporation, has no plants or offices that employ more than 150 people.

The founder believed that 150 was the maximum number of first names a person could refer to comfortably.

I know of a high school with 2,200 students. At a faculty awards dinner, the principal had to introduce faculty members to each other although they had worked in the same building for three and four years. We have built school buildings that are too large in order to save money and, as a result, spend more money trying to solve communication problems. Smallness uncomplicates communication.

D. Standardization of Operations

Structural point of view. Given the common structure of middle and large school districts, it is impossible to expect that all teachers in the same subject at the same grade level will teach the same exact subject matter in the same general style at approximately the same time. Loosely coupled systems—and school districts are prime examples—should not expect conformity among professional people. One of two things is called for: (a) Release teachers from the expectation of conformity and live with diversity (which denies the traditional roles of supervisors and the rules of curricular scope and sequence) or (b) assume that the unit of instructional quality control is the school building (placing central office curriculum and instruction people in an advisory/consulting role).

E. Parental Complaints Based on Comparative Programs

Structural point of view. If districts have organized parent groups, PTAs, or whatever, on a districtwide basis, then parents expect districtwide parity. If districts have distributed districtwide curriculum guides, brochures about "the district," or similar "report cards"; employ a district public relations person; or disseminate a district newsletter and other centralized communications to parents—*then parents will expect sameness in all schools.* If you have conditioned parents to think as a district, they will. This is a problem caused by structure. Restructured districts can educate parents differently.

F. *The Difficulty of Distributing Sparse Amounts of Public Funds Equally*

Structural point of view. Changing the central administration of funds may be the most difficult part of restructuring. All schools cannot be equal and therefore, in any given year, the needs are different. Who determines the needs? If that process is centralized, then the district will have problems and complaints when cuts are necessary. You can distribute funds and assign cuts equally to all schools, but the impact is not equal because their perspective of needs naturally is different. More decentralized distribution of funds, as long as it is basically equal by student count, will allow more building-level freedom and consequently less hassles with the budget office.

G. *Unproductive Principals*

Structural point of view. The problem is simple: In most districts, performance supervision is too far removed to be effective. Do not attempt to control principals from the district office —which is often spoken of in terms of "being a team player." A principal should be responsible for his or her building, and if the building is not productive, the principal should be removed. The only reason the system has a few productive principals is because those principals have shown personal initiative and this initiative is not related to district performance review policies. If superintendents believe their productive principals exist because superintendents have exercised tight controls, they are kidding themselves.

H. *Relationship Problems Between District Staff and Building-Level Administrators*

Structural point of view. Teachers, custodians, cooks, and others literally have two bosses in most school districts' tables of organization. These two "bosses"—one at the building level and one from the district office—have overlapping duties. Conflict management can be a positive force in organizations. The problem is that traditional school organization patterns were designed in the belief that conflict could be controlled or minimized.

I. Low Morale, High Stress

Structural point of view. Low morale and its frequent companion, stress, accompany large, bureaucratic, impersonal organizations. That's one of the reasons many corporations have taken steps to decentralize. If the communication system between teachers and the district office is earmarked with memos, directives, newsletters, and large group meetings, there will be a morale and stress problem. Decentralized systems have less organizational stress and higher morale generally.

J. Creating Representative Mechanisms Has Not Had the Expected Payoff

Structural point of view. Representative democracy works for the United States of America, but direct democracy works better in professional/organizational environments. Attempting to get the proper mix of representatives, relying on them to actually represent their constituents, assuming they report back to their group accurately, and hoping the large group is satisfied with input is wishful dreaming. Large, centralized organizational systems' attempts at token representation exhibit structural weaknesses.

K. Environmental Responsiveness

Structural point of view. Modern textbooks in organizational theory describe the current way of looking at organizations as "open systems." Organizations more than ever before are affected by and affect people, groups of people, and other organizations as well as the government. This happens in ways not understood by earlier theorists. The point is that whatever unit of organization that presents itself to the environment is the unit that interacts. The problem with loosely coupled organization patterns in the school system is that it is very difficult to control or anticipate environmental interactions. Thus boards of education and superintendents are accused of being slow or nonresponsive to needs, suggestions, and complaints from their constituents. Problems occur in the school buildings, but solutions seldom occur if managed from the central office. Further, communicating possible solutions to the community tends to miss the mark. Patterns such as school site management allow schools to relate directly to their immediate environment.

L. *Principals' Role Conflict*

Structural point of view. The educational literature has been replete with an emphasis on principals as strong instructional leaders. Many principals, in an attempt to live up to those expectations, however, are frustrated because their job descriptions allow for very little freedom to create, innovate, plan for change, fire incompetent teachers, or, in general, manage their shop. Placing middle managers in key roles to enforce productivity and then withholding authority is a weakness of the current school district structure. This is true even if the principal only imagines he or she is restricted. Visibly augment the principal's authority and free the principal to lead the instructional program!

M. *Achievement Test Scores Are Still Low*

Structural point of view. Past management systems allowed several unfortunate things to happen to schools.

- Educational managers did not create accountability systems.
- Legislatures and the community faced with this void forced standardized testing on the schools.
- Educational managers allowed these testing programs to be the only measurement of achievement.
- Now it is almost too late to educate the public about alternative methods of accountability.

All of these situations occurred while districts were in their current centralized patterns. Attempts to significantly raise standardized achievement scores have failed, and will continue to fail, because the organizational culture is slow to change. Smaller units of workers can supply evidence of their individual achievements much more easily.

In consultation with parents, on-site managers can devise measurement techniques that are unique to their situations. We will never show "success" under our current management system. It is self-destructive.

1.3 Look at Your Table of Organization: This Is Your Enemy

Look at your table of organization. Chances are that it looks something like a triangle or a pyramid. (See Figure 1.1.)

We must all realize that public schools have copied their governance systems from nineteenth-century organizations such as the military and efficiency-based corporations. Now, even the military and most corporations have adjusted their structure so that it is more flexible, adaptable, and "down powered" than before. It is interesting to note that, in the 1991 Middle East war between Iraq and U.S. and coalition forces, a remarkable difference in military governance was identified. In general, the Iraqi forces were controlled from a very centralized philosophy, whereas the American forces had been trained so that if company and unit commanders lost communication with headquarters, they were to continue to act on their own and follow the plan. When the Iraqi communication lines between headquarters and field commanders were destroyed by coalition forces, the Iraqi field commanders were immobilized because they were afraid to act independently. This difference in mobilizing forces became a significant factor in the outcome of the war, which favored the coalition's decentralized forces.

A most important assumption about the old pyramid structure of organizations was the historic supervisor-employee ratio. That ratio was always established as 1 supervisor to 7 employees. Under those conditions, the hierarchical approach has a reasonable chance of succeeding. There is no way that public

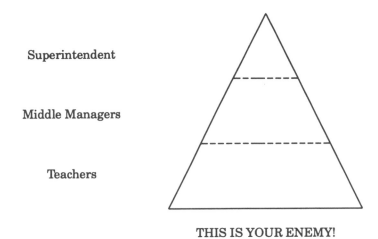

Superintendent

Middle Managers

Teachers

THIS IS YOUR ENEMY!

Figure 1.1. Organizational Pyramid

schools will ever have that kind of supervisory ratio because of financial limitations. We have added district office personnel to assist in supervision but they do not come close to filling the large gap. The ratio for most public schools is at least 20 to 1, in some situations rising to 50 or more to 1. The hierarchical, pyramid structure designed for business, industry, military, and the Catholic church will not work in public schools.

A realistic design looks more like that in Figure 1.2 (*notice the relative position of teachers*).

The problems of the pyramid design are illustrated in the following counterproductive scenarios:

Dependency. Decision making becomes painfully slow because administrators at various levels are waiting for permission to act. Slow decision making creates a cumbersome organization.

Hot spots. Given the traditional organizational structure, certain positions in the organization become hot spots; that is, these positions are bottlenecks in the decision-making/communication process. These positions vary from district to district depending on

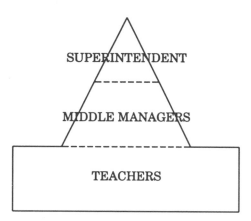

Figure 1.2. Realistic Organizational Design

the circumstances, but examples might be the director of secondary education or the business manager. These positions can easily become funnels that create tension up and down the line.

End-run syndrome. Personnel at all levels and of various personalities soon learn to "end run" the table of organization and its chain of command to talk or plead at the next step up. Thus they skip levels, sometimes going directly to the board of education. If the pyramid worked, this would not be necessary. The form does not fit the function, so people create devices of their own, such as the end run, to accomplish professional goals.

Pockets of isolation. Some positions and some functions are never integrated into the mainstream of the management process. Examples might be the business office, which seems to ignore program needs, or a small department like special education that isolates itself. The larger the district, the more pockets we find. These pockets may contain people with valuable expertise that is thus underdeveloped.

Micro management. Micro management occurs when higher-level managers and/or the school board interfere with lower-level functions. The structure, due to distance from the action, creates impatience with and mistrust of subordinates. This is somewhat the reverse of the end-run syndrome in that the organizational table is ignored and interventions are made at improper levels regardless of standard procedures.

Squeaky wheel syndrome. Parity and efficiency break down because some people are more persuasive than others. The typical organizational table is based on assumptions of rationality when in fact school systems are nonrational.

"They said" syndrome. The organization is too large to deal with personal concerns so executives are seen as the "generalized other," which shows up in conversation as *"They* said . . ." or "What are *they* doing now?" Executives become nonpersons. Employees become bitter.

Goal displacement. Effort is misdirected at procedures to attain ultimate goals as opposed to efforts that directly result in goal attainment. We know this syndrome as the "red tape" that distracts us from our mission.[1]

Create systems that are capable of change and possess greater authenticity of purpose and behavior. Power down!

1.4 What Is Restructuring?

I have studied the recent literature pertaining to restructuring so that I can provide readers with a knowledge base from which to converse with constituents regarding the definition of and need for restructuring. Table 1.1 is a meta-analysis created for this purpose. The horizontal names represent recent (within two years) opinions of experts and theory about restructuring (authors are in the reference material) and the vertical represents characteristics mentioned in the literature. The resulting matrix provides a "picture" of the popular meaning of restructuring.

The most popular conception of restructuring is that it means decentralization followed by professionalism, which is related to empowerment—next on the list. Student learning outcomes and better use of instructional time are the next most frequently

TABLE 1.1 Meta-Analysis of Restructuring

Factors Include Characteristics, Components, Goals	Jenkins	O'Neil	Brandt	Roebeck	MacPhail	Brickley	Bailey	Tyack	Lewis	Elmore	Edwards	Neuman	Lieberman	Rauth	Timar	Rayuid	*Totals*
Mission/outcomes	X														X		2
Student learning and intellectual development				X		X		X	X			X	X		X		7 student learning (4)
Character development				X		X											2
Personalizing education						X					X						2
Collegiality, empower, shared decision		X			X	X	X		X	X	X				X	X	9 empowerment (3)
Instructional use of time		X	X			X					X	X					5 use of time (5)
Integrated learning						X						X					2
Interactive learning						X						X					2
Application of technology					X	X											2
Accountability	X	X			X	X			X							X	5 accountability (5)

Column group heading: *Authors* (Jenkins through Rayuid)

														Total
Structural decentralization	X	X	X		X	X	X	X		X	X	X	X	12 decentralization (1)
Flexible use of resources			X						X					2
Profession staff development team leader	X	X	X	X	X	X				X	X			10 professionalism (2)
Self-change and renewal	X	X			X									3
Collaboration and partnerships	X						X	X						3
Student involvement and freedom						X	X							2
Parental and community involvement					X				X	X	X			4
Contract negotiations and unions				X								X		2
Political process					X	X						X		3

15

mentioned items. The next characteristic of note is that restructuring means improved accountability. Other characteristics are
scattered in terms of frequency and are not significant for this study.

So there you have it. Why restructure? To decentralize, to
gain professionalism, and to empower. These changes will improve accountability, student learning, and use of time. All of
these characteristics will provide the educational system with
increased adaptability to change. Evolutionarily speaking, sur-
vival depends upon adaptability. Why restructure? We do not
want to be the dinosaurs of the twentieth century.

1.5 What Are the Options?

Restructuring requires rethinking. Restructuring requires a
shift in paradigms. Restructuring is *not* keeping the old order
in place and reshuffling some activities; neither is it about a
new public relations campaign that only touches the surface. If
a district is serious about fundamental changes, there are many
options to consider.

The first level of options, if you want to improve schooling,
involves looking at your school system's current organization.
Harold Leavitt (1980) has a simplified schema for looking at any
organization. The schema illustrates the four major components
to any organization: task, structure, technology, and people.
Look at Figure 1.3 and evaluate your organization.

For years, educators have been trying to redefine the *task*
(mission and goals) of education. Although we still need to work
on this component, I "score" the *task* component of public education as an accomplishment. We are still searching for clarification.

In terms of *people,* we have seen constant staff development
energies applied—I think with considerable success. We have
good, qualified people who had good preservice education and
good in-service training. We have spent a lot of money on this
factor and are reasonably successful. I give *people* a plus score.

The *technology,* of course, is being developed constantly.
Education's "technology" is pedagogy, and we have made vast

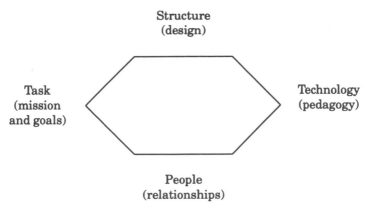

Figure 1.3. Harold Leavitt's Theory of Organizations
SOURCE: Modified from Leavitt (1980).

improvements in the science of learning and teaching in the last two decades. I score the *technology* of education with a plus.

We have spent time, money, and energy on school improvement projects with seemingly very little success. A change in the fundamental *structure* of our public schools is the only way we are going to get fundamental changes that have an impact on outcomes. I score the *structure* component with a minus because we have not adjusted structure since the early twentieth century.

What is the second level of options within the restructuring continuum? Figure 1.4 describes these options. Maintaining the status quo and faking restructuring are really not viable options. Site improvement activities with increases in the committee structure do not going far enough. Not too many people in public education speak seriously about voucher plans although they are a restructuring option. What about choice? It appears to be successful in several states but, of course, choice involves broad commitment from the state and local boards and remains controversial.

But we can have school site management without the controversy of choice. There are implementation options within the broad definition of site- or school-based management. Table 1.2 outlines three possibilities of implementation—pilot school,

Degrees ←——————→ Process	
Status quo	Continued loss of effectiveness
Site improvement	Increased quality and quantity of committee structure
School site management	LEA management process (a) pilot school (b) readiness proposals (c) simultaneous implementation
Choice	School board, community, and state involvement
Vouchers	Referendum and state legislated

Figure 1.4. Restructuring Continuum

readiness proposals, and simultaneous implementation—and describes the pros and cons of each.

If a district chooses the pilot school approach, the main advantage is that it is a conservative tactic and mistakes can be corrected more readily. The major problem is that there will be some confusion in district office roles. The other more important problem is that pilot programs are intended to be trial programs and must be evaluated at the end of a prescribed period. The problem then is evaluation. Does the district have the resources to measure progress adequately?

The readiness proposal type establishes the criteria for conversion to school site management when the school is ready. The school submits a proposal to the district office to gain approval. The major problem to be dealt with in this situation is that the district will have to maintain two governance systems at the same time: one that controls traditionally and one that enables individual buildings to self-govern (within limits). This plan is safer than wholesale shifts, however, because control is still being exercised.

Simultaneous implementation may be the best choice if there is reasonable openness and readiness for the change district-wide. It is also important that ample preparation time is given.

TABLE 1.2 School Site Management/Site-Based Management

Management Choices	Pros	Cons
Pilot school	Cautious	District office roles? Evaluation and generalization
Readiness proposals	Conservative Readiness	District office dual systems
Simultaneous implementation	Coordinated single system	Threatening Concentrated staff development

The simultaneous plan may have a difficult budget impact during the given implementation year. The simultaneous option requires a concentrated staff development plan over a fairly short period of time.

What is best for your district? The next chapter will outline various strategies to implement restructuring.

Review of Key Concepts

❑ Current organizational design is an impediment to educational reform.

❑ The most common views of restructuring include decentralization, professionalism and empowerment, and improved learning outcomes.

❑ Organizations are composed of tasks, people, technologies, and structures. Of these, *structure* needs our priority attention.

❑ Restructuring can be viewed as a continuum along which school site management accomplishes the most for the amount of effort extended.

❑ School site management can be implemented as a pilot school, simultaneously, or through readiness proposals.

Note

1. My thanks to Dr. Joe Jennelle of the Christiana School District (Delaware) for his help with some of these concepts.

References

Bailey, W. J. (1991). *School-site management applied.* Lancaster, PA: Technomic.

Brandt, R. (Ed.). (1988). *Content of the curriculum.* Alexandria, VA: Association for Supervision and Curriculum Development (ASCD).

Brickley, D., & Westerberg, T. (1990). Restructuring a comprehensive high school. *Educational Leadership, 47*(17), 31-38.

Cohee, W. (1991). *An analysis of negotiations* (Executive Position Paper). Newark: University of Delaware.

Edwards, J. (1991). To teach responsibility bring back the Dalton Plan. *Phi Delta Kappan, 72*(5), 398-401.

Elmore, R., and Associates. (1990). *Restructuring schools.* San Francisco: Jossey-Bass.

Jenkins, K. (1991). *A comprehensive view of restructuring.* Unpublished manuscript, Appalachian State University, NC.

Leavitt, H. J. (1980). On the design part of organizational design. In H. J. Leavitt, L. R. Pondy, & D. M. Boje (Eds.), *Readings in managerial psychology.* Chicago: University of Chicago Press.

Lewis, J., Jr. (1983). *Long range and short range planning for educational administrators.* Boston: Allyn & Bacon.

Lieberman, A., & Miller, L. (1989). Restructuring schools: What matters and what works. *Phi Delta Kappan, 71*(10), 759-764.

MacPhail-Wilcox, B. (1990). Project design: Reforming structure and process. *Educational Leadership, 47*(17), 22-25.

Neuman, F. (1991). Linking restructuring to authentic student achievement. *Phi Delta Kappan, 72*(6), 458-463.

O'Neil, J. (1990). Piecing together the restructuring puzzle. *Educational Leadership, 47*(7), 4-10.

Rauth, M. (1990). Exploring heresy in collective bargaining and school restructuring. *Phi Delta Kappan, 71*(10), 781-790.

Raywid, M. A. (1990). Rethinking school governance. In R. Elmore (Ed.), *Restructuring schools.* San Francisco: Jossey-Bass.

Roebeck, B. (1990). Transformation of a middle school. *Educational Leadership, 47*(7), 18-21.

Timar, T. (1989, December). The politics of school restructuring. *Phi Delta Kappan,* 265-275.

Tyack, D. (1990). Restructuring in historical perspective: Tinkering toward utopia. *Teachers College Record, 92*(2), 170-190.

2

How to Restructure a School System

2.1 Decentralize Management Functions

Once a school district has made the philosophical paradigm shift toward decentralization, the next concern is to decide how to restructure. Planning should involve looking at the major management functions and how might they be changed. Possible functions to consider are listed below. They are listed in the order of their importance.

A. *Functions*

Districtwide organizational goals and individual school building goals and objectives are the first areas to consider. Remember that, although the district's overall mission has not changed, district and school building goals were written in a context of centralized organizational assumptions: We can make the change or set new goals because we have the supervisory staff, knowledgeable central office people, and enough money. Times are changing so that those old assumptions may not be valid. School building goals may shift under a restructured organization. Because mission statements, goals, and objectives are the first consideration in developing any organization, these conceptual guidelines should be the first to be considered under restructuring.

B. *Accountability*

Accountability will be covered in several other sections in the book but, as part of this management function list, accountability is perhaps the biggest change in the restructuring process. With a shift downward in responsibility, the people in the individual school building will have more to say about accountability. Almost by definition, building-level accountability measures will differ or vary slightly from building to building. That is one of the reasons that the districtwide goal setting process is so very important. Schools must follow district guidelines. To what extent are you willing to let buildings deviate from "the average" in setting goals and reporting the results?

C. *Curriculum*

Deciding what curriculum is written, taught, and tested obviously is important. Restructuring may mean that grade levels and buildings may differ slightly in terms of their curriculum. For example, the district has a goal of "writing across the curriculum." All teachers must help students improve their writing, but each school may go about meeting that goal in a slightly different way. State requirements have to be either followed or changed.

D. *Instructional Supervision*

The next chapter will outline one answer to this difficult problem but, if the role of the central office supervisor is changing, then it is time to change the managerial function. For the most part, supervision can be done at the building level.

E. *Budget and Financing*

Centralizing this area is a real test for the board and superintendent. Care must be taken that there is equal distribution of funds to students under the law, but, in general, a larger percentage of fund expenditures will be decided at the building level. The powering down process will raise morale, but there will be arguments.

F. *Discipline*

Because discipline and order are such important parts of schooling, this item is high on the list. Are there any discipline rules or procedures that should be kept at the central office level? Most of the policies and decisions, and the application of policy, can be determined at the building level. The reason this works is because discipline and behavior are such a part of a school's ethos. Climate is related to student morale, which is related to discipline. What are the cultural conditions at each school? The faculty and staff can create their own policies.

G. *Parental Involvement*

For the most part, we have viewed parental involvement in two ways: individual teacher contact with a student's parent or districtwide programs such as PTA, advisory councils, and district committees. Now we must look at parental involvement where it will make a difference—in the school building. The questions center on what flexibility will be extended to principals, and what mechanisms will help this function of decentralization work? For example, school building advisory councils are recommended.

H. *Personnel*

One could restructure and leave the personnel office intact. Certain personnel functions are dictated by law, and conformity is necessary. I would say anything not bound by law should be part of building-level responsibility. For example, let's review the hiring of teachers. They must be certified according to state requirements, equal opportunity legislation must be followed, fringe benefits and their distribution become law, and so on. But the selection of teachers from short lists of qualified teachers is certainly a building province.

I. Extracurricular Activities

Does your district employ a person who coordinates athletic contests, the hiring of coaches, scheduling, and the like? This is no longer necessary. Can you live with the fact that one high school in the district sponsors a girl's volley ball team and one does not. If the district is not in violation of Title IX provisions, then the answer should be "yes." Do the marching band, cheerleaders, gate receipts, and coaches salaries have to be the governed in the same way? Are they now?

J. Support Services

For the most part, support services—that is, cafeteria, maintenance, custodial, transportation, and in some cases library services, nursing, counseling, and audiovisual—are centralized functions. They have been routinized in that fashion for a very good reason. The reason has been from a motive of efficiency. But efficiency is not nearly important as effectiveness. Effectiveness is managed best from smaller units of control. Will there be some waste through overlap of duties? The answer is "yes." Will there be higher morale in these buildings? The answer is "yes." Will there be confusion in the beginning? The answer is "yes."

K. Public Relations

What is past practice? How can it be changed? It does not make too much sense to me to have someone at the central office writing in a district newsletter about school site management. School building personnel know what is going on in their school.

To have this function stay at the central office is efficient. To delegate it downward is effective.

Once it has been determined what changes are going to be made with each of these functions, the big question is this: When will these changes be made? The two options are (a) simultaneously, with giant efforts to train, announce, educate, implement, and evaluate all at the same time, or (b) in rank order, in terms of timing criteria and transferring authority gradually. Each district's decision makers must decide this based on readiness factors.

2.2 Solve Effectiveness Problems With School Site Management

Patterson, Purkey, and Parker (1986), in a significant analysis of school systems, delineated the following problems facing most school districts: demographic changes, federal and state demands, growth in community expectations, constant fiscal crises, impact of collecting bargaining, decline in quality and quantity of teachers, and declining sense of efficacy. They point out that the rational, bureaucratic system that has evolved is not effective in dealing with these huge problems. The answer is to restructure, to reduce a rationally structured system into smaller organizational sizes. These small units, primarily a school building or a school within a school in large high schools, can be monitored, controlled, planned, and evaluated in a way that is effective. Sometimes large school systems can be efficient; they are hardly ever effective. Assuming Patterson et al. are correct, we look at their list of problems and see "a declining sense of efficacy," "decline in quality of teachers," "community expectations," and "demographic changes" as problems that are more easily dealt with by smaller units.

Efficacy is accomplished by successfully bringing together Leavitt's four components, which were mentioned in Chapter 1. They are task, technology, people, and structure. We have discussed the elements of structure, but all four of these must be activated in concert if the organization is to gain effectiveness.

School building administrators can deal with the people in the building in a personal, meaningful way if the people view the building as the place where they work, get their assignments, get evaluated, and have a share in governance.

The tasks, missions, goals, and objectives of an organization can never be fully achieved unless the people have a sense of ownership and understand this mission and school philosophy. Talking about a school district's goals is usually too remote for most classroom teachers because "it is *their* problem" (meaning the district office). Talking about *our* school's goals is less abstract and thus more attainable.

The technology (pedagogy) may not vary as much as the other components except in one very important way. The energy, motivation, and enthusiasm that a teacher demonstrates in delivering a new curriculum or a new instructional technique makes all the difference in the world. For example, under the efficiency model, the district decides to introduce cooperative learning in all classrooms. There is a districtwide workshop required of all teachers to learn the new methods. Evaluation checklists are modified to include this new technique. Right away, you have a morale problem. If you have a morale problem, you have a lack of effectiveness.

Now consider this scene. A school within a school that houses 200 students each with nine teachers has a series of staff development meetings in which new ideas are discussed. They democratically decide that, of the new instructional ideas, cooperative learning holds the most promise for their unit. They request training and implement the new ideas—constantly sharing with each other the progress or lack of it. They modify their plans quickly when needed. Now, in which of the two school settings would you rather have a child of yours placed?

Efficiency models focus on the following:

centralized purchasing
standard curriculum
comprehensive programs
certification
accreditation

common teacher evaluation forms
focus on time (schedules, contact hours, working hours,
    and so on)
departmentalized disciplines
accountability
salary schedules
constant discussion over methodology

The above are important. Effectiveness models, however, focus on the following:

decentralized purchasing (decisions at the work group level)
flexible curriculum to meet individual differences
personalized programs
small teams of teachers with power
teachers viewed as decision makers
teachers viewed as researchers
evaluation through management by objectives (MBO) and
    portfolio
process oriented
concern for climate
differentiated salary schedules
situational methodology

Effectiveness is defined as doing the right things. *Efficiency* is doing things right. We need both, but form (efficiency) follows function (effectiveness). The general concepts of school site management provide for the effectiveness model without necessarily losing ground in efficiency.

2.3 Decision Criteria

There are several factors to consider before beginning to restructure. They are discussed below.

A. *Readiness*

Someone has to determine if there is a general readiness on the part of the primary stakeholders to accept restructuring. This status is difficult to determine. Informal chatting with teacher and administrator groups, straightforward discussions with union leaders, surveys of teachers and parents, observing reactions to the new plans at meetings, and meeting with small groups of influence leaders will provide the collective feedback that is essential. The readiness factor really deals with the psychological and philosophical aspects of implementation. Chapter 6 on "change" will discuss this in greater detail. But, at this point, ask the question, "What is the general sense of the employees regarding the change?" There will always be "resistors" and "early adapters." The decision makers need to be concerned with the middle third of the teachers' group who are "on the fence." When the majority of the fence sitters seem to agree with the change, *act!*

B. *Budget/Finance Considerations*

The budget director will have to agree to change purchasing, procurement, budgeting, inventory, and like services. Adherence to state laws must be maintained. Larger amounts of monies will be granted in block form to the individual schools. Is there a willingness on the part of principals to accept these duties? Is there a willingness on the part of the budget office to relinquish these responsibilities and power?

C. *Staff Development Plan*

An estimate of plans and costs for staff development must be calculated prior to implementation. Principals need support, central office personnel may need to be retrained, and teachers will need to prepare for their new roles. One way to plan for the costs of restructuring staff development is to divert all staff development monies toward restructuring. All authorities seem to agree on one thing, which is that training must accompany decentralized restructuring.

D. *Accountability System*

Everyone is concerned about accountability. The trouble is that we have spent considerable time arguing about districtwide accountability without much headway. Now, we must think about individual school building accountability. I doubt if we will get away from district-level accountability requirements, but new ways to measure progress in individual buildings must be added. Some of these methods are building-level goal setting, outcome or school success indicators, academic indicators, and contracts. These are discussed in detail in Chapter 7.

E. *Instructional Supervision*

Who supervises instruction now? How might this change? Are the new role players ready? Are the old role players willing? Is there a need to change?

F. *Marketing Plan*

This concept could be controversial because school district public relations departments have spent a lot of time and "copy" explaining how all of the schools were basically the same. Now, by definition, a decentralized system of schools promotes diversity and differences. This requires a paradigm shift on the part of the parents and taxpayers. So the concept must be sold. Information about individual schools must be disseminated, and evaluation results must be distributed in a different light. Each district must decide the extreme to which they are willing to take this factor.

G. *Teacher Evaluation System*

It is entirely within reason to establish variations of the teacher evaluation system among schools. After all, if you allow more freedom to schools for their own marketing plan, curriculum modifications, budget, and staff development, then there may be a need to develop separate teacher evaluation systems in each school. Evaluation systems organized around specific building needs and updated every year should be more helpful in improving instruction than centralized systems covering all grade levels, subjects, and disciplines.

H. Implementation Schedule

A series of events must occur as the implementation plan takes hold. Without action plans before start-up, the mission will fail. This is not something you play by ear and "see how it goes." It takes very careful planning and timing. Every school district has a current system of governance. Now, under restructuring, this system is going to be changed. This transition period between the two systems may be hectic because, for a period of time, there will be dual systems for accountability, budgeting, and so on. The complete conversion process might take three years. One year or less is too quick. More than three years drags things out and there is a loss of momentum.

I. Involvement Plans

The following stakeholders must be involved to some extent: school board, administrators, teachers (individuals), teachers (association), support personnel, parents, and taxpayers. Each group deserves special planning attention. Obviously, the board is the priority. The board of education must be convinced so they in turn can "sell" the idea and plans to others. The matrix in Figure 2.1 can be used in this decision process.

2.4 What Must Be Done at the School Building Level to Accomplish Restructuring?

My review of the literature on restructuring revealed that, for most experts, restructuring means decentralization. The school building in a decentralized organization of a system of schools is affected the most. What must be done at the school building level to accomplish restructuring?

Each district must decide the extent to which the district is to decentralize. Also, each school may differ in their timing and the completeness of restructuring. In any event, the following factors must be dealt with at the building level.

Criteria	Acceptance Degrees (check status)				
	1 *(not ready)*	2 *(under discussion)*	3 *(50% ready)*	4 *(positive feeling)*	5 *(approved)*
Philosophical readiness					
Budget/ finance					
Instructional supervision					
Accountability system					
Marketing plan					
Teacher evaluation system					
Implementation schedule					
Involvement plans					
Totals					

Figure 2.1. School Site Management Decision Criteria Matrix

A. *Training and Development*

At a midsize school district that was attempting to restructure, the assistant superintendent for instruction decided to shift the normal methods of staff development planning and funding.

Previously, the central office staff budgeted, planned, implemented, and evaluated all professional development activities. Four of the fourteen principals in the district refused (or attempted to refuse) these "block" funds as well as the responsibility that went with the funds. The assistant superintendent finally insisted and the staff development process is now a building-level responsibility throughout the district.

In that little scenario, there is a very telling story that is indicative of the problems in education. Because, we have controlled matters from the top for so long, the on-line managers don't know how to handle a change.

If a school building has been given approval to take over the training and development function of the district, then they must plan well for those scarce funds. An example process might look like this:

What Are the Building's Needs?

- Determine the needs through participative methods. This should include the principal's ideas as well. The participative methods might include surveys, focus groups, task force meetings, and suggestion boxes.
- Organize a planning group or use the existing shared decision-making body to draw up plans to meet these needs.
- Compute the costs of the staff development plan.
- Determine the budget through normal building priority setting.
- Send the proposal to the central office for final approval. (Note, this step can be eliminated if agreed upon earlier.)
- Activate the plan.
- Evaluate the activities immediately following and at the end of the year.

B. New Role Assimilation

Because each building in a system of schools will have variations in objectives and goals, the administrators must discuss their new roles. These activities might include small discussion/ counseling groups, meetings with union officials, faculty meetings with and without the principal, like groups from other schools, and administrative council meetings. More details are provided in Chapter 3 and 4 but, in general, the potential shifts are as follows.

Teachers will share more general decision making on the obvious issues of curriculum, instruction, scheduling, material acquisition, and discipline. Principals and assistant principals will share decision making with teachers. At first, this may seem inefficient. It may always be inefficient. But what we are after here is effectiveness.

The concept of differentiated staffing will come into play in these discussions. The differentiated staff idea has been around a long time and will discussed later in the book.

If we started education over again and assigned educators to school buildings and told them to organize their school so that it was effective, I don't believe we would come up with the current configurations. We would look at the functions that are necessary and look at the human resources and deploy them in a flexible ways so that some would teach, some would help with the budget, some would write curriculum, and some would monitor study halls. The jobs would vary according to needs of the day, week, and year. But, to have this kind of flexibility, the unions must back off; the school board must be open-minded; the central office must give a little; and the superintendent must learn to manage more like a college president and less like a corporate executive.

The largest role change will be with the principal because he or she has to assume some of the duties previously handled by the central office. They will have to learn to be group facilitators, influential leaders, and controllers.

c. Decide on Decision Making

There is a chance that, at the building level, planning and decision making have not been shared. Sharing was unnecessary because the principal was responsible for these functions. Most buildings have committees working on various topics, but restructuring affects building governance. This is a large role change.

The principal, perhaps with central office approval, has to decide on a decision-making procedure for the building. What are the options? Although one would hope each building would arrange a unique, creative approach to this problem, there are a few models.

1. *Quality circle(s)*: These will be explained in Chapter 3.
2. *Administrative councils*: These are representative groups that include administrators with teacher representatives. Members are usually appointed.
3. *Senates*: A senate is usually composed of representative teachers with one or two administrators invited, and all major decisions would come through this group for action. Members are usually elected.
4. *Faculty vote*: This is a variation of the old monthly faculty meeting. The difference would be in the frequency of meetings and in topic selection.
5. *Advisory group or groups*: Although not a new idea, advisory groups democratize the school if the principal abides by the group's recommendation at least 80% of the time.
6. *Combination of one or more of the above.*

The point is that the decision-making process needs a lot of study. Decisions on decision-making procedures should also be shared, and, whatever process is used, it must be fully understood by all concerned.

D. *Building Personnel Accountability Plans*

The employees in any given school building must be held accountable for their performance. The plan used can be different than that used in other buildings within the district. This may be difficult to imagine because we are so used to waiting for orders from the central office or from the state. First, how are individuals or groups of work-alike personnel going to be evaluated? Second, how is this information reported to the person concerned and to the organization. The school may need to change to professional systems such as Management by Objectives (MBO) and/or portfolios (Shulman, 1991).

E. *Budget Management*

Plans must be made for budgeting and purchasing. Most states have very specific guidelines to cover the minimal accounting procedures, and sophisticated districts have developed additional policies. First, what policies can be legally changed to allow for more discretion at the local level? Second, what are the new procedures for budgeting going to be at the building level? Do not proceed to restructure until these details are worked out. The entire budgeting process can be downshifted, or parts (e.g., staff development) can be delegated. Records of expenditures can be kept at the computer center of the district office, but the budget process needs to be established at the building level with whatever monies are available. Of course, all buildings should receive the same amount of monies per student.

F. *Determination of Discipline Codes*

Each building, advisedly, in connection with representative parents, must establish their unique discipline codes. Does the school want a liberal policy that emphasizes self-discipline, growth, and educative methods or does the school want a very structured system of rules and regulations and a punishment system to accompany them? This decision must coincide with the goals and objectives of the individual school. Taxpayers are particularly concerned about discipline in the public schools because they hear the bad news from the media. School site management will fail if there is a perception that discipline is weak or inconsistent.

G. *Curriculum and Instruction*

Traditionally, curriculum and instruction have been the prerogative of the state or county or district. Under restructuring, much of this responsibility will be delegated to the school buildings. Before restructuring takes place, mechanisms need to be in place to manage curriculum, curriculum development, curriculum evaluation, testing, and instruction. Each district must decide what portion of these responsibilities will be left to the individual school and which ones will be shared or kept by the central office. Because many teachers have relied on central administrators to keep them informed of curricular trends, they may resist involvement at first. They will say they don't want this curriculum responsibility, they don't know enough, or they don't have time. Eventually, when the average teacher sees that there is a payoff, that what he or she does makes a difference, he or she will cooperate with the decentralized plans. But this will take time. District office curriculum people become resource consultants under these decentralized plans. Within each school, the faculty must decide who is going to control the curriculum.

If topics are planned and acted on prior to the actual shift of governance, then that shift will run much more smoothly. That is not to say it will ever be smooth, but eventually the discussions and debates will be primarily located in an organizational unit small enough and motivated enough to make better decisions and implement them enthusiastically.

2.5 What Must Be Done at the Central Office to Accomplish Restructuring?

Depending on the size of the district and the existing ethos, restructuring the district office may be the most difficult of all of the changes. When the experts talk about decentralizing, they are referring to many roles previously played by district office supervisors and administrators. Whether these people are line or staff may not affect their natural fear of being replaced. In fact, in some districts, restructuring has resulted in a few supervisors being reassigned to local schools. Central office people rarely lose their jobs or even take a pay cut, but their job descriptions may change rather drastically. Communicating with district office personnel early in the discussion sessions may reduce anxiety as well as increase early involvement in decision making regarding prospective changes. The task at hand, making schooling more effective, however, is a higher calling than protecting the egos of a few administrators. Specifically, the issues that must be dealt with are as follows.

A. *Change the Name of the Central Office*

The image of the command center must be changed as well as its principal functions. *Education center, resource building, internal consultant's office,* or *educational assistance center* are all better names. The new role for the district office may be more like that of the county or regional service center that is present in some states. Changing the name in the direction of service is an important step.

B. *Establish Time Lines*

The time necessary to completely restructure is difficult to predict. Several authorities, however, have suggested a three-year period. Even then the move will not be successful unless there are careful time lines and target dates established. If these specific dates are missed, they can be adjusted, but the important things are (a) to move fast enough so that the move does not lose momentum and people's interest and (b) to move slowly enough so that the majority are supportive.

C. *Revitalize Roles*

The district office decision makers need to implement a process of role revitalization. These role changes can be coordinated by district office staff (someone at the district level established them in the first place), but they involve or can involve everyone including support personnel as well as teachers and administrators. New job descriptions need to be written and a new table of organization needs to be designed that recognizes these new roles.

D. *Identify Specific Skills and Expertise Among District Staff and Market Them to the School Buildings*

Some can help with budget preparation, some can teach others to write grants, some can write curriculum for the local schools, some can assist in the observation/evaluation of teachers using the school building's system. Prepare an internal consultant book or brochure that advertises the skills of all personnel not directly assigned to a school building. Let these supervisors respond to requests for help in their areas. The superintendent will soon know who the valuable people are in the new central office role.

E. *Agree on a Performance Review System*

The old way of evaluating central office staff may not be applicable anymore. What are their new roles? How do you want them to be evaluated? I would suspect part of the new evaluation would include some feedback from the people in the schools who might have used their talents and can speak specifically about them.

F. *Training and Development*

Just as the school buildings need to develop their own training and development programs, so does the district office. For example, someone could provide workshops on how to be a consultant or someone else could go back to graduate school and learn new areas (a federal projects coordinator learns more about general budgeting and offers his or her expertise to the committee in a school). Now, instead of thinking about a staff development plan for the whole district, the plans become quite specific.

G. *Reduce Requests to Principals*

As soon as the initial talks start, the work load of the building principals starts to increase. To alleviate some of that work load while the district is operating under two systems, district office personnel must reduce the number of requests sent to principals that require a response. These are very time-consuming.

As an example, in one district where I consulted, the director of research started going to the buildings to look for and prepare data for various state and district reports. Heretofore, this data had come to the district office at the request of the director. Have principals make a list of all the reports, surveys, and oral requests that they must handle. Go through that list and reduce it by at least 50%. The school will still get along.

What can you do tomorrow to start powering down? Chapter 3 explains how to empower faculty.

Review of Key Concepts

❑ Decentralizing involves analyzing key management functions and determining where new responsibilities fall.

❑ Factors to consider before restructuring include readiness, budget, staff development, accountability, instructional supervision, marketing, teacher evaluation, scheduling, and plans for involvement.

❑ Each school building personnel must collaboratively decide what must be done at the school level to achieve an effective transition.

❑ Changes in roles at the district office must also include minimizing the quantity of requests to principals.

References

Patterson, J. L., Purkey, S. C., & Parker, J. V. (1986). *Productive school systems for a nonrational world.* Alexandria, VA: Association for Supervision and Curriculum Development (ASCD).

Shulman, L. (1991, April). *Teacher improvement.* Paper presented to North Carolina State University, Raleigh.

3

How to Empower Faculty

3.1 Let's Talk About Governance

In earlier chapters, I emphasized structure as an organizational factor. I hope the case made for decentralizing that structure was effective. Coordinating the components of organizations (task, people, technology, and structure) are the function of governance. Power is what makes governance work. One definition of power is the ability to predict outcomes. In other words, if one has power, one can manage the governance system in a way that ensures effectiveness.

An effective school is one in which learning is taking place. Learning cannot take place unless the teachers are effective.

For the most part, teachers will be effective if they share in the decision-making process because they will feel ownership in their professional job. Along with shared decision making comes shared responsibility, which some teachers will be reluctant to assume. With proper training, faculty development, and the appropriate leadership style, however, most teachers will respond in a favorable manner. Top-down power has been demonstrated to be unresponsive to the never-ending changes and challenges of our society and educational community. "Powering down" or empowering may be the last hope for public education. Empowerment is an effective model. Students will achieve if teachers are empowered. A structured curriculum with the proper scope and sequence and standardized guidelines is simply no substitute for individual teacher enthusiasm, creativity, and professional pride. Therein lies our choice. Do you want to continue with the efficient, logical curricula produced by the state or do you want turned-on students who love school, learning, and themselves?

3.2 Preparing Teachers for New Roles

Generally, there is little from teachers' preservice training that prepares them for this new role as empowered professionals. There is apt to be very little from their service experiences that prepares them, except in some isolated, smaller districts and one-room schools. Furthermore, there is not much help from current in-service training. Although the basic function of instruction will be the same for many teachers, there will be role changes if a school site plan is to work effectively. How do we prepare teachers for these new roles?

First of all, what are the new roles? The roles will vary from school to school, but we might expect the teacher of a school-size plan to accomplish the following (Bailey, 1991):

1. Set personal, professional goals that are well written, measurable, and applicable to the goals of the unit, school, and district.

2. Converse with the principal regarding these goals and be able to convince the principal that the goals have been accomplished.

3. Be the primary contact person with parents of the children in her or his unit.

4. Be a spokesperson for the school work site. Conduct oneself as a proud member of that work site and be a good liaison between the school and the public.

5. Be prepared to chair efficient and effective team meetings as well as participate in a mutual work-sharing process.

6. Serve on decision-making teams for the school and be trained in the various methods of group decision making.

7. Be a competent judge of curricular materials. Know how to select, implement, and evaluate curricular materials.

8. Serve as a peer coach.

9. Serve as a peer evaluator making the best use of the school's evaluation system and observation techniques while assuming an objective and professional stance.

10. Be familiar with a variety of instructional techniques including knowing which techniques work best with which students and knowing when to use each technique.

11. Be able to defend these new roles objectively and intelligently to parents.

12. Have an understanding of standardized tests, when to use them, and how to interpret them.

13. Be a subject matter specialist in one or more areas.

14. Be a generalist educator.

15. Construct in-house tests for subject matter achievement.

16. Write instructional objectives to cover major subjects.

17. Manage unit budgets.

18. Supervise student teachers.

19. Serve as a mentor to new teachers.

20. Hire new teachers as part of a screening team.

21. Be computer literate.

22. Be able to conduct and teach library research.

23. Remain up to date on education, instruction, and education policy trends.

Each building's staff will make their own list of role expectations, and we can expect this to be a complicated process with considerable conflict. There will be arguments from the teachers union, from teachers who will claim "that's not what I was hired for," from some who are threatened by the whole process, and, yes, from a large group who want more money. To the latter, the answer is probably, "We can't give you more money, but we can give you more respect." Again, each building, with careful leadership and training and development activities, can resolve these issues. As previously stated, this process may take about three years. There is no hurry, but please get on with it.

Next, how do we organize teachers in an empowered system?

3.3 Assigning Building-Level Work Teams

School site management is one way to decentralize restructuring. Empowerment takes the restructuring a step further and allows professional faculty members the professional freedom they deserve. The building principal, however, needs a plan or an organizational structure within the building to organize these professionals. It is my contention that the best way to empower teachers and still provide a quality control system is to develop work teams of three, four, or five teachers who have common interests. Thus decisions about the learning environment are made by these working groups as long as the decisions are in keeping with the law and district policies. A variety of organizations both in the public sector and in private corporations have begun to use small work groups as the basis of their organizational structure. The experience is that quality control can be built in through peer pressure; motivation and morale are higher; and individuals who are members of a group take pride in their work as well as the group's productivity.

Albert Shanker (1988), president of the American Federation of Teachers, has stated that he does not believe improvement efforts directed toward masses of teachers will have sufficient impact because of the basic isolation of the classroom teacher. He has supported school site management and empowered groups of teachers because those plans tend to enhance the position of teachers and teaching. The primary location for professional interaction can only be at the building level because teachers are geographically close enough to interact on a daily basis.

These work groups can be labeled *teams,* although this kind of group is not to be confused with team teaching. Team teaching could be more easily accomplished if small work-alike groups had already been established, but the work groups I am referring to do not necessarily have to teach simultaneously. How do we form these groups?

The principal and/or a planning committee need to look at their schools demographics and make locally based decisions about these kinds of assignments, understanding that they should be flexible so that changes and modifications can be made with minimal fuss.

The factors to consider are as follows:

- School philosophy, long-term goals, and annual objectives
- Grade levels
- Degrees of self-contained and subject specialties
- Size of school and size of normal teaching groups or classrooms
- Composition of faculty experience
- Strengths and weaknesses of the instructional program
- Faculty compatibility
- Amount of training time and money available
- An organizational evaluation plan in place

Examples of work groups follow:

- A primary school has four natural fourth-grade classrooms. Unless some factors such as compatibility are serious deterrents, the work team would be those four fourth-grade, self-contained teachers.
- A middle school has assigned teachers to subject area specializations. There are three people who share the math-science teaching for these middle grades. They form a working team.

- A small high school has one art teacher, one music teacher, and one home economics teacher. They form a team.
- A large high school has an English department with 20 faculty. They arrange their group into four groups of 5 or five groups of 4.
- A middle school has six teachers of special education. They assign one special education teacher to one, two, or maybe three groups of other teaching areas so they become resource teachers for that team *or* all six special education teachers form a team and implement their curriculum.
- Professional support personnel (nurses, counselors, school psychologists, home and school advisers, and so on) need to be placed in a work group as well. They can be organized as a group (support personnel) or they can be spread around among the other work groups.

Having to make the decision about assigning professionals to work groups will cause or perhaps "force" school-based decision makers to look at their goals and particular needs at that school. Work group assignments are not to be taken lightly because they will make a difference, if groups are given proper autonomy. There should be some group with central authority within the school such as a curriculum council that will approve each group's annual plans or of any major changes in curriculum or instruction. Some districts will want a district office group to approve changes at certain levels, but caution must be exercised. Remember, we are trying to reduce bureaucratic procedures. In review, remember that form must follow function: What are we trying to accomplish? What kinds of faculty groupings will allow us to accomplish our objectives and to be ready and able to make adjustments in those groupings?

3.4 Developing Small Group Decision Styles

Empowerment will work best if teachers are assigned to work-alike groups, but these groups will not work well unless they plan carefully about how the group will make decisions.

Most groups have difficulty with planning for and acting on decision making. A day or two of training in small group dynamics, small group process, and small group decision styles will be sufficient and is well worth the time, money, and energy. Just because professionals are intelligent and well meaning does not mean they are prepared for the interaction of decision making. Either an internal consultant or an external consultant can help prepare them.

Perhaps the most important point to have understood is that there are many ways groups can make decisions, and voting is usually not one of the best methods. David W. Johnson and Frank P. Johnson (1975) have developed categories of decision making that are outlined below, with some modification.

A. *Authority Rule Without Discussion*

This is best used when there is an administrative need for simple routine decisions, information, and plans. It can be used by the team leader as previously agreed upon and might apply to setting meeting times and dates, handling correspondence, communicating with the principal, or when members are absent. The disadvantages are lack of involvement, but there are times, hopefully preagreed, when involvement is not necessary.

B. *Expert*

This method is useful when one member's experience far outweighs that of anyone else in the group. It might apply to a special knowledge that one teacher has about a specific child or a subject matter specialty. In this case, the "expert" informs the group about what is best and the group follows up on the decision because they have trust in this method for very specific situations. The difficulty may come in declaring who is an expert.

C. *Average of Members' Opinions*

This is not voting. My version of this Johnson and Johnson category is to ask: "What do you guys think?" The leader quickly takes a poll of most of the members' opinions on a matter and, based on the results, proceeds with a plan. It is useful when there is a shortage of time, when it is difficult to have all members present, and when the outcome is not crucial. If done too hurriedly or too frequently, there may be unresolved conflict that might hamper group cohesiveness.

D. *Authority Rule After Discussion*

This method uses the resources of the group more than previous methods and the discussion could be helpful for group understanding, but, of course, it does not build any real commitment and is not the best method for most cohort groups. This method is more applicable to an administrative advisory group than it is to a collegial work-alike group.

E. *Majority Control*

Majority control is another name for what most groups think of as voting. If a group does vote, then they must predetermine what constitutes a decision: simple majority, two thirds, or whatever. The disadvantage is commitment from the minority. Remember, if you use a simple majority rule—for example, five people vote, with two against and three for—there could be significant percentage (40%) who are going to be a problem during implementation. The vote is best used when a decision is forced on the group and consensus has not worked even after repeated tries.

F. *Consensus*

Real consensus takes time in many cases and some groups do not have the patience for this method. Many times the term *consensus* is used incorrectly. Consensus means: (a) Everyone has expressed his or her opinion (this is different than everyone just having a chance to express an opinion) and (b) everyone agrees on the same course, plan, decision, or inaction. The disadvantage, other than time, is that you can have a "hung jury." If one member is opposed to proposition X, then the group cannot proceed. Some groups with a high degree of trust can get around one member's opposition by asking carefully and without pressure if the one "no vote" can agree to "go along" with the decision of the group *and* he or she can agree to abide by the outcome as if he or she were in favor. The important part is that everyone has expressed his or her opinion. The consensus method is the best method for most small professional work groups.

G. *Nominal Method*

The nominal method is not covered by Johnson and Johnson but is basically a numerical system that is used frequently in quality circles. This is a structured approach that is usually not necessary for small groups but is a good way to allow for all to speak their opinion but also to arrive at a close decision. The actual procedure can be done several ways. The most common version is explained in the section on quality circles. The general idea is to ask members to rank order the available options and, through simple arithmetic, a priority emerges.

Each work group, after having understood the decision-making options available to them, must choose which methods they are going to use for which kinds of decisions. This must be done in advance of actual decision meetings. The lack of a clear-cut decision-making process is responsible for most misunderstandings and ineffective small group meetings.

3.5 Implementing Quality Circles

One very successful method of empowering faculty is through the use of quality circles, which is explained in detail by Bailey (1991); however, there are several variations. Briefly, a quality circle is a meeting of small group(s) of members of the faculty and support personnel to influence the administrative decisions of the school. The two basic organizational options are these: (a) Each work group is a "quality circle" (QC) or uses the methods of quality circles, or (b) there can be a representative group elected by the faculty that is charged with dealing with specific issues concerning the life of the school.

Included in the original concept of the quality circle was the idea that the circle replaces the quality control supervisor in industrial settings. Production units learned that they got better quality if the workers were involved in the quality control process. The original quality control circle did not make management decisions but made recommendations to the bosses about work improvement ideas. The concept has worked well in education (Bailey, 1991). One of the decisions that a school must make is whether the circle is going to make management decisions or whether it is going to make recommendations to the principal.

The following is an example of how this might work in a school. Summer training is held for the actual participants in the circle. Prior to this training, the entire faculty elected representatives to serve on the QC in a rotating three-year cycle. Two of the six members will leave after the first year and will be replaced, and so on. The group is from a small middle school with a faculty of 30. The people designated to replace the first two also attend the workshops. As a result of the training, a plan is created, which, with the principal's approval, is outlined as follows:

1. The QC will be announced as a prestigious and important recommendation body for the school.
2. It will not replace any of the other standing or ad hoc committees.
3. The QC meetings will take place during the school day, which means the principal must free teachers, aides, parents, and volunteers for these meetings. Sometimes substitutes will be used to cover classes.
4. The group has decided that no meetings will last more than 50 minutes.
5. There will be a meeting every week except those preceding holidays.
6. Every member of the group has a specialized job in addition to being a voting member. The roles they assume are as follows:

Facilitator: Conducts the meetings in the prescribed fashion and makes sure the meeting time is not exceeded.

Recorder: Takes minutes of important decisions and reports them to the principal and the faculty at large.

Disseminator: Takes responsibility to produce a QC newsletter that is issued at least twice a month, which, in addition to the minutes from previous meetings, contains process observations as well as items discussed and not acted on, and encourages faculty to submit their problems and suggestions.

Researchers: Collect information for groups to use in decision-making processes. Two people serve as in-house researchers. When the group decides on an issue and wants more information upon which to make the decision, the group asks the researchers to do library research and documentation studies, conduct surveys, do interviews, and fact find. These reports are submitted to the QC.

Reporter: Reports to the principal after every meeting the recommendations that are forthcoming and their rationale and takes ideas and responses back to the QC from the principal.

7. Bylaws are written that describe QC membership, decision-making procedures, data collection, dissemination proceedings, and other matters of some permanency.

8. Part of the bylaws contain policies as to permissible topics for the group as well as topics that are out-of-bounds. For example, they decide that any matters relating to curriculum, instruction, and curriculum materials are permissible topics. They decide that personnel matters that involve career decisions for individual teachers are off limits and the responsibility of the administration.

9. They establish several procedures by which the group can receive input from the faculty. The procedures are as follows:
   ideas from regular faculty meetings that can be referred
   a suggestion box just for the QC
   team meeting agenda items
   principal input
   individual contact between the faculty at large and QC members

10. They decide to use the decision-making model provided by the consultant, which is the nominal method. The meeting format agenda is as follows:

Quality Circle Decision-Making Process

(1) Recent input	10	minutes
(2) Choose and define problem (rank order)	10	minutes
(3) Brainstorm causes	5	minutes
(4) Select viable solution options	10	minutes
(5) Discussion Research when more information is needed	5 to 15	minutes
(6) Prioritize solutions	5	minutes

Meeting Total Time = 35 to 50 Minutes

(7) Make recommendations to the decision maker
(8) Disseminate information
(9) Evaluate
(10) Repeat cycle

Important Points on Starting a Meeting

- The leader studies and understands the technique and provides pads and pencils for each participant and a large pad of newsprint on an easel. A calculator is also handy to have.
- The problems to be approached are presented in a clear, brisk manner; for example: There is too much noise in the hallways.
- With problems listed, the leader asks each participant to offer a single response and continues in a round-robin fashion until all responses are placed on the newsprint for all to see.
- The members are allowed to clarify the items listed. The items are not debated. Every response is treated as a serious and important item.
- Next, members are requested to choose a number of items (for example, seven items of those listed) that they feel to

be important to them. They write these items on another piece of paper.

- The leader than polls the group and records how many times each item was chosen.
- It will become apparent that certain items are chosen more often than others. Those chosen most often are listed on the newsprint.
- Participants are asked to study this new list and to place the items they feel are most important in priority order.
- When the group has finished this task, the leader records the number of participants assigned to those items they chose. By adding the numbers, the group decides the priority of the items most important to it.

They are now ready to solve the problem they have chosen, and so on.

There are external consultants who can come to the school setting or a faculty member can get training elsewhere and bring it back to his or her colleagues. A strict adherence to "the quality circle guidelines" will promote continued interest and faith in the empowerment process. So many attempts to empower break down because of either the principal's lack of faith in the participative process or, more often, a breakdown in the decision-making process. When the procedures of a meeting get sloppy, people lose interest. Process is everything.

3.6 Leading an Empowered System by Including the Work of Team Leaders

There are two basic leadership roles in an empowered school. The leadership behavior of the principal and other administrators is crucial to the undertaking, and the leadership ability at the teacher-peer level has a direct relationship to the success of self-governance. The literature is replete with research, theory, and advice about leadership, leadership skills, and leader impact, and sometimes this can be confusing to the practicing administrator who has to be a leader on a daily basis.

Yukl (1981) has synthesized these various authorities as well as anyone else and reports the following traits and skills that are generic to leadership in general. I have added the particular behaviors that will facilitate a participative style:

Yukl	*Participative Leadership*
Managerial motivation	Motivated for high-involvement management
Self-confidence	Confidence "spreading" to confidence in faculty and shared decisions
Energy level	Participative leadership takes more time and energy than other styles
Emotional maturity	Only the mature can delegate and empower with success
Technical skills	In this case, technically skilled in group process as well as other processes
Human relation skills	Conflict management, counseling techniques, facilitator skills, verbal communication, and listening skills
Conceptual skills	Must understand and convey concepts of shared decision making, small group process, school site management collegiality, and joint "ownership"

The leadership style of a team leader is less well defined, and very little research has been done at the school site. Other than his or her own commonsense group process skills, the team leader must elicit from the group what they want in terms of leadership. In other words, in my view, each team leader may perform different leadership tasks and behave in various ways as modified by the work group. The group then needs to look at their charge, which will vary from school to school, and outline their functions. Sample functions are to call meetings, lead meetings, and decide on decision methods, topics to be covered, evaluation of the program, and the group process—and then decide which of these will be the responsibility of the team leader. All of this process preparation takes time and will be very frustrating to many. The leadership role is crucial, however, and, in an empowered school, is best decided by the group. As one can see, this is a whole new ball game of striving for effectiveness and minimizing the urge to be only efficient, the way most of us were trained.

Someone in the school—the principal, administrative council, or quality circle—must accommodate the following concepts of a well-led organization:

- The school must be goal directed; that is, there are a stated mission, long-range goals, and annual objectives understood by all.
- However decisions get made and whoever makes them, the decisions should be data based, objective, measurable, and evaluated.
- Programs, curriculum, individual students and groups of students, faculty, administrators, and the restructuring process itself *must be evaluated at regular intervals*. If educators don't evaluate their progress, someone else will and it won't be helpful.
- The organization, through leadership, must be flexible and ready to change and adapt to educational trends and the socioeconomic needs of the community it serves.

If there are overall plans from leadership to accomplish the above and if specific leadership roles within the school have been carefully delineated and trained for, restructuring will work.

3.7 Alternative Ways to Proceed Toward Empowerment

The following case studies will illuminate alternative methods a district might deploy in a move toward an empowered district. All of the scenarios are from real situations (either observed by me or from consultants). The districts remain anonymous.

A. *Case 1: "The Serendipity Approach"*

Case 1 is about a district in the Northeast. It is basically suburban, with a "pie-shaped" sector reaching into a city that was desegregated by court order a decade ago. There are approximately 14,000 students grades K to 12. The new superintendent was instructionally oriented and had promised the board of education she would focus on instruction and work at raising achievement scores while insisting on sound discipline in the schools. The superintendent was intellectually attracted to school site management as a means to improve test scores, deal with the increasing multicultural population at the grass-roots level, and cut back on costs at the same time.

The state in which she operated had just inaugurated an early retirement system for teachers and administrators. About six administrators with district office assignments elected to retire. In most cases, the superintendent did not view this loss as negative.

Her plan was as follows: Take advantage of the vacant positions and streamline the district office by down powering functions to the building level. Plan a two-day administrative retreat and invite key board members, parents, and teacher representatives to the retreat. Employ an external consultant to present a workshop on the advantages of school site management. Give a personal address at the workshop (some 40 people) of the new vision for the district. There would be school site management, there would be a new table of organization, the district was going to deal with district diversity in this new plan, and, following planning sessions at the workshop, a new plan and long-range goals would be presented to the board within a few months. The superintendent knew that most board members would go along with the restructuring. The teacher representative saw this as an opportunity to empower teachers, and most of the players were in place.

With a summer to plan and with two pilot schools that had been operating as empowered schools for two years as models, the plan went into action within two years of conception. The change model was this: "As any building is ready for school-based management, they [faculty and administrators] will present their plan to the administrative council for approval." The plan is working, with several schools applying each year. It is anticipated that within a four-year frame, from beginning to end, the district will be successfully restructured.

B. Case 2: "The Long Slow Curve Approach"

In this case, the superintendent would like to "spark-up" his school district. The district, located in the South, with a strong state department of public instruction, has encouraged districts to decentralize through permissive state legislation. This mid-size district has been pursuing school site management in a very gradual process. Some line item accounts in the central budget have been turned over to the principals for their discretion. For example, the staff development budget was delegated to each principal. Some of the principals either did not like that responsibility or did not know what to do with it.

Without any official decree and without making it an issue with the board of education, the superintendent is making small, quiet moves toward providing principals with more responsibility. No central office people will lose their jobs, nor are they apt to have a serious change in job description. A one-day workshop was held with all administrators (no board members, no parents, and no teachers) to help principals understand their new role and to help train them for it. This rate of change will probably go on for three or four years until a degree of decentralization is accomplished that satisfies the superintendent and the three assistant superintendents. Empowerment of teachers is just as slow and low key. Some principals with training are working on quality circles and other empowerment devices to assist in this low-key restructuring. Given the political situation the superintendent has with his board of education and the apparent willingness of the administrators to go along with these subtle changes, this seems to be a reasonable path for this district.

c. Case 3: "The All Together Now Approach"

This case involves a sophisticated school district in the Mid-Atlantic states area that is primarily suburban in nature. School site management, like all other changes, will be very well thought out and routinized. The district will be restructured in an orderly fashion with guidelines, workshops, goal statements, and teacher union involvement. All schools will be given more responsibility at identical levels and expectations. All teachers will be empowered through an official and standard districtwide procedure of elections among building faculty, the formation of identical administrative councils, common voting procedures, and standard means of parent involvement. In other words, this is a very orderly, highly managed system of empowerment. The union is involved and changes have been made to the union work agreement contract. Parents are involved in more depth than before; each building will have a parent advisory council that will have districtwide bylaws. Some supervisors were moved to the building level, and other central office employees have formed a task force support group to aid individual schools. Schools who want assistance must fill out the required requisitions and wait for approval. To some extent, regardless of the well-managed aspects of this district's empowerment process, they have exchanged one set of bureaucratic rules and regulations for another. They have spent a lot of money on retraining, research, publicity, and realignment of the curriculum. They have a quality control system built in. Time will tell if they are any better off than before.

In reviewing these different methods of empowerment, several questions must be asked of all three districts:

1. In fact, are teachers any more empowered than they were before? Do they *feel* empowered?
2. Is there an evaluation plan in effect that will provide indicators that the restructuring activities have improved schooling? (From a consultant's point of view, this is the most difficult requirement to get across.)

3. What are the long-range implications? Is anything really different or is this another educational trend that will pass with time?
4. Is there a spirit of professionalism and high morale throughout the district?

Ask your "district" these questions.
Now let's look at "increasing professionalism" in Chapter 4.

Review of Key Concepts

❑ Powering down or empowerment may be the last hope for public schools.
❑ Teachers must be prepared for their new roles through staff development.
❑ The best way to empower teachers and still provide a quality control system is to develop work teams of three, four, or five teachers who have common interests.
❑ Small work groups must decide on a decision-making process for their group.
❑ Quality circles have much to offer a restructured school.
❑ The various leadership roles within a school must be delineated, developed, and evaluated regularly.

References

Bailey, W. J. (1991). *School-site management applied.* Lancaster, PA: Technomic.
Johnson, D. W., & Johnson, F. P. (1975). *Joining together: Group theory and group skills.* Englewood Cliffs, NJ: Prentice-Hall.
Shanker, A. (1988, November). Speech delivered to the NCISE National Convention, New Orleans.
Yukl, G. A. (1981). *Leadership in organizations.* Englewood Cliffs, NJ: Prentice-Hall.

4

Increase Professionalism
Through Empowerment

4.1 Power Is the Only Thing That Multiplies
When It Is Divided

Someone said that power is the only thing that multiplies when
it is divided. Yet public school administrators have been reluctant to share power. The meaning of the expression is clear. If
subordinates in an organization have power that has been delegated to them, they feel stronger and are more involved in their
jobs. This increases the total power available in the organization. Thus to empower is to delegate or "power down" to the level
of teachers to give them the professional respect they deserve.
The accountability measures that are discussed in this book can

be employed, so there should be no fear of misguided teachers. If people have a belief that they have ownership in an enterprise, they will be reluctant to deviate from the norm. If people believe that what they do does not make a difference, they will find ways to sabotage the system.

Critics of the current system have constantly pleaded for teacher empowerment, but school administrators have been reluctant to delegate, and many teachers have been reluctant to cooperate with power-sharing attempts. Part of this situation is fed by the structural problems we have discussed before. But this combination of empowerment, along with restructuring, is not only inviting, it may be the last hope for public schools as we know them. "Effective schools" are not enough; we need excellent schools. The only way to achieve excellent schools is to have excellent teachers. The only way to have excellent teachers is to give them the power to be real professionals. Let the power multiply.

The issue has been identified by Shedd and Bacharach (1991, p. 1):

What has been identified as a second wave of reform has coalesced around three propositions: Teachers are not (but ought to be) treated as professionals; schools are (and ought not to be) top-heavy bureaucracies; and no significant improvements can occur in America's systems of public education unless schools are fundamentally restructured.

The problem is this: What kind of restructuring and what kind of empowerment? What does it really mean to empower teachers? Thus the philosophical issue becomes a very practical problem.

People continue to debate the general criteria of a professional, and teaching is no exception in this debate. Hall (1975) submits that there are three groups of characteristics of professionalism that can be measured. They are structural criteria (formalized code of ethics and prescribed training process); attitudinal attributes of members (belief in service, self-regulation, and autonomy); and societal recognition (society in general viewing the occupation with respect). Because it might be difficult for any employee of an organization to meet all of these criteria, the issue boils down to the way employees are treated within their organization. This is the call for empowerment. If administrators treat teachers as if they were professionals, then they are professionals. If they feel and think like professionals, they will begin to take on the characteristics illuminated by Hall.

Clearly, professionalism in most organizations is something into which one grows. Teachers need help and encouragement in this attempt to grow into professionals. When they can improve their training and entrance requirements, and create a general attitude about their work that is self-regulatory, then society will have a greater respect for teachers.

Generally, increasing professionalism means extending involvement in the decisions and planning activities of the organization. Shedd and Bacharach (1991, p. 130) report a synthesis of various research projects, which state that involvement in management can increase job satisfaction, reduce role conflict, raise morale and trust, reduce stress, and contribute to successful change activities.

Teachers can be empowered as individuals, as small work groups, or/and as representatives of the rank and file. The kinds of activities, areas delegated, and forms of empowerment with all three of the above categories can vary widely. Choosing areas in which to "power down" is a sensitive issue. Administrators who command that "tomorrow all teachers will design their own curriculum" are missing the boat. Administrators who call teachers together and ask, "What are the priority areas in which you would prefer to be involved?" are stepping into the boat of progress. What are some specific ways in which teachers can be empowered?

4.2 Using Teachers as Researchers

If teachers were engaged in research and scholarly pursuits such as professors in universities, they would be respected more by society and probably have a better attitude about their power over their own destinies. I assume most teachers would have to have expanded training in research. But how is this to work, given that teachers are overextended in work assignments now?

The classroom teacher is a manager and observer of the classroom environment, which includes people, learning materials, facilities, and the psychological as well as the physical climate. Excellent teachers are very aware of these environmental conditions. How does the aware teacher determine the effectiveness of these conditions? How does the excellent teacher make changes for the better with regard to these variables? What should this professional change within that classroom environment to make improvements?

A professional teacher will know because he or she will collect data that bear on those outcomes. This "research" may be clinical (experience); it may be experimental (control groups and so on); it may be ethnographic (observations of the group dynamics); or it may be quantitative (test score comparisons). All of these minitechniques of scholarly behavior can be taught in undergraduate classes, in graduate schools, or through staff development activities.

The question is *not*: Can the average teacher conduct site-based research on her or his classroom? The question is this: Where are the reward systems for doing so? In a restructured system of schools, teachers are viewed with respect in terms of their current knowledge, their source of knowledge (research), and their application of research in the classroom. Administrators need to provide time, training, rewards, and encouragement for the new public school teacher. I don't believe it is too much to ask. Let's look at some examples.

Example 1. Instead of receiving her master's degree in a standard subject like elementary education, Mary took her graduate work in research methods. In the restructured system, the principal assigned Mary to be test score coordinator for the school. He gave her two released hours of teaching per week for this work. The time did not cover all of her efforts but it served as a recognition reward. She was given access to the school's best computer and, in addition to becoming test coordinator for the school, she helped individual teachers with item analysis so they could work on deficiencies within their classes. These teachers found her role in this regard to be less threatening than that of the previous districtwide coordinator. Mary chairs a testing/research committee that is responsible for making recommendations to the schools' curriculum task force for improvement. The data she collects are site based, nonthreatening, and appropriate for the school's immediate consumption. Mary is rewarded on the merit pay scale for this "administrative work" because of her contributions to the school.

Example 2. John has always been fascinated by learning styles. He has taken several graduate courses in cognition, learning styles, and alternative teaching strategies. The school paid his tuition because it was part of his personal improvement plan, his MBOs, and his department's goals. With permission from 90% of the high school parents, he has administered several standard tests that predict learning style. He also wrote an abbreviated test form that he hopes to get published. Armed with these style data, John has modified his instruction (of high school algebra) to suit these style needs. He keeps accurate records of progress on each student. He devised several innovative methods of instruction to accommodate his program of individual instruction. Several teachers have copied these methods because he reports his work several times a year to the faculty research committee and through the faculty newsletter. He is working on an article reporting his positive results. When asked how he finds time to take on these additional duties, his response is that he feels so involved in what he is doing and that he has been given the freedom to vary his teaching program that he does not mind. John is a "turned-on" and empowered teacher. He was invited to study for his doctorate in a nearby university with the promise of an eventual college teaching position and he declined. His current professional work is very rewarding to him. He is paid to lead a summer workshop on learning styles, which earns him recognition and extra income.

Example 3. Sally teaches science in a middle school. She is a team leader of the science-math group that writes and tests the science and math curriculum. She is concerned about the great volume of literature that is being published on science, scientific methodology, and middle school instruction research. The team asked her if she would take on the responsibility of locating, reading, evaluating, condensing, and applying this abundance of information on a regular basis. The team has "traded" some of the members' normal duties for this service she provides and the principal provides a substitute once a month so that she can visit the university library. The school has given her a computer with distance networking capacity so that she is connected with a group of scholars across the country who talk to each other electronically. As a consequence, she has become invaluable to curriculum development in the school and is invited to serve on summer workshop staffs, through which she earns additional income. A middle school journal has commissioned her to write a column each month, and they pay a small stipend. Sally has endeared herself to the faculty, most of whom refer to her as "professor." She loves the recognition. The district offered an early retirement plan recently for which she was eligible, and she said "nothing doing."

4.3 Differentiated Empowerment

Managing power and structure is serious business. When Norman Cousins discovered he had a very serious disease years ago, he said this is too serious to be left to the doctors. He proceeded to develop his own cures in addition to the standard medical care; and his "cure" is now legendary. Perhaps the business of school improvement is too serious to leave to the politicians, professors, and administrators. The teaching profession must apply their experiences and knowledge to the situation as well.

Lee Shulman stated in a speech in 1991 that we cannot mandate or legislate excellence: "The only way to improve standards is by local building initiatives and classroom teacher efforts." If the secret to better teaching is the teachers, then the question becomes, "How do we free them so they can in fact be better?" They need two kinds of freedom. They need academic freedom, which provides for the psychological motivation of being in charge and knowing they have to deliver, and they need structural freedom, which comes from restructuring and empowerment. Specifically, they need time to plan, discuss, research, evaluate, and manage. And how do we buy them time? It's simple. We have had a conceptual device to rearrange the teacher's role for at least three decades.

It's called "differentiated staffing." Remember the 1960s and Fenwick English's plea for us to look at teaching in other than unitary roles? Do you remember the mid-1980s and the rush toward career ladders? Career ladders are a spin-off of differentiated staffing, but the general failure of both of these movements has left us without imagination about school improvement. There are logical ways to defy the homogenization of teachers. Of course, the teachers unions have had a retarding effect upon differentiating a faculty. This has been a sensitive issue, and it becomes associated with merit pay, which gets criticized because "we don't have adequate means of evaluating teaching." But we are talking about restructuring and empowerment because the old, traditional, homogenized ways have not worked well enough to satisfy the American public, let alone the professional critics. What is differentiated staffing or what I now call "differentiated empowerment"?

Differentiated empowerment is a management device to apply specialization and motivation to the teaching act and to the management of schools. Do teachers really make equal contributions to a school? No, effort and substance differ as a natural human function. Can all teachers handle all of the duties associated with teaching equally well? No, the concept of the unitary teacher—that is, one teacher who is interchangeable with any other teacher—is dead. Differentiated empowerment, on the other hand, looks at the functions that have to be performed and at staffing resources and creates the best job match possible. These jobs can be associated with career ladders and merit pay, or the salary schedule can remain unchanged. Some districts will not want to differentiate salaries, but most schools are able to make job assignments that are differentiated. The problem here is not unions, contracts, or seniority but simply a conceptual one. Empowerment means rethinking faculty functions, job descriptions, and school effectiveness.

Some of the "jobs" that might be assumed by the classroom teacher include team leadership, curriculum development and curriculum materials writing, counseling students, planning, budgeting, parental associations and contacts, discipline coordination, mentoring new teachers, faculty study groups, in-house research projects, hiring and screening committees, or testing coordination.

Some differentiated plans designate "master teachers," with or without extra pay. It is a motivational device designed to have holding power for the very good and experienced teacher who might move to another school or another occupation.

However plausible differentiated plans sound, a great degree of sensitivity must be exercised in changing from the old, homogenized system to one with an empowered staff with flexible positions. After all, there is some security in knowing what your job is and what you have to do every day. But that security factor is exactly the problem. Teachers, in their classroom isolation booths, are restricted in their views of the larger needs of the school. Differentiated empowerment is one way to minimize the isolation, to motivate teachers to take a larger view of education and to professionalize their jobs. This change process must include the teachers. Task forces to look at the changes, liaison with union groups, and trial periods are recommended. The planning will take about two years, and there will be conflict. The desired result is *not* to have teachers feel impotent. Empowerment is about challenging tradition.

What are the practical problems of freeing classroom teachers from their student responsibilities to perform some of the aforementioned "administrative" duties? Each school will have to problem-solve this one, but the following will get us started:

- Consider summer (full-time) pay for those teachers who want it.
- Use the technology that is now available to us with innovations such as distance learning, programmed instruction, computer-based instruction, and cooperative learning (one teacher can supervise more groups for a short period).

- Team teaching, which distinguishes styles of teaching (large group, small group, individual study), can free some teachers for short periods of time.
- Create longer school days for certain teachers who would have to be paid additional income.
- Expand use of paraprofessionals, teaching aides, and the like. There are simply many functions that the teacher performs that can be handled by uncredentialed personnel.
- Administrators and support personnel can have teaching assignments. In addition to freeing teachers, this is a great morale booster for teachers, and it helps develop a spirit of camaraderie for all.
- Junior and senior high schools with designated planning periods can do creative things with that time slot. For example, complete teams of teachers can be scheduled for their planning period at the same time.
- Pay substitute teachers to relieve teachers for these duties. They are hired for field trips, why not this?
- Use parent volunteers. With training, there are a lot of jobs that parents can do.
- Convince the school board or the state that there is nothing sacred about 180 days of school; 175 days of schooling or 170 days of schooling, for example, will not change achievement scores, but several days for planning will transform the effectiveness of most schools. This time could be in the form of one afternoon per week.
- Maybe precious staff development (in-service days) should be used for these purposes. Evaluate the current in-service days and see what the teachers think of that use of time.

Some of these suggestions will require state exemptions, some will require district policy changes, some will require altered union contracts, and some will require a change in the teacher's formal contract, but the only thing that really is required is a change in thinking about schooling. Empowerment will work with some work. (Note: Those who want more information on differentiated staffing and career ladders should refer to Edelfelt, 1985, pp. 62-66.)

4.4 Developing Self-Policing Behaviors

A professional is a member of an occupational group that polices itself. Everyone knows about lawyers and the bar association, doctors and their boards, and plumbers and their licensing. In each case, members of these occupations help develop standards of behavior for their group. In this sense, teachers do not meet this criterion for a being professional. But why not? If the structure is decentralized and teachers are truly empowered, then for the first time we could have forms of professional monitoring. One principal with 40 teachers cannot be a constant enforcer of so many employees. What are the ways in which teachers could learn to self-police?

The first area was discussed earlier, and it is ethics. Acting in terms of agreed-upon behaviors is a form of self-policing. The second way is through professional organizations such as associations and unions. These groups can provide partial quality control over their members. We have examples of that now but this process needs extension and more sophistication. The third way is through performance review systems that involve fellow members of the profession in evaluating formative and summative performances. This latter can be in the form of peer coaching, shared observations, committee review, and other devices that look at the contribution made.

In other words, there is the individual teacher and her or his sense of efficacy and high morals. There are small groups of work teams that can police each other because they are concerned about the production of their team. Then there are policing behaviors that are organized by large associations. This issue is more philosophical then real at this writing because it is difficult to implement policy on such a wide scale. The important thing here is that supervisory policing has not worked (look at the poor test results and critical national reports). True professionals establish their own rules, regulations, licensing, and so on. Wake up educators—take your lives in your own hands in the twenty-first century.

4.5 Speaking to Unions

There are basically three views about teacher unions. The first is that teachers never should have been organized in the first place and that unions are not professional and should be dissolved as soon as possible. The second is just the opposite, that is, unions are the savior of what we now have that's positive and, without them in the future, teachers will lose more ground in the race for economic recognition. The third view is somewhat of a compromise. It holds that unions may have had their place historically, but, if unions are to have any impact in the future, they are going to have to change their basic function. I ascribe to this latter view. If unions want to stay in business and if they are going to make a contribution to education and society, then they must change their role.

Shedd and Bacharach (1991, p. 166) state: "The most distinctive pressure is to include teachers in the formulation of educational policy and programs, which necessarily involves a redefinition of the roles that boards of education, administrators, teachers, and their representatives play in the management of school systems." Shedd and Bacharach continue their argument by pointing out that collective bargaining in education is itself undergoing major changes, just as educational systems are, and that it will be gradually restructured to meet the needs of a restructured school system. The authors continue:

> Rather than being adversarial and concerned with preserving their own power, the new unions will be cooperative and non-confrontational. Rather than oppose efforts to improve the quality of teaching, they will actually assume responsibility for the quality and quantity of their members' efforts. Rather than negotiating rules that restrict flexibility, they will look for ways to relax restrictions on both teachers and administrators. Rather than insisting that teachers' rights and benefits be allocated equally or else on the basis of seniority, they will insist that the responsibility and compensation of teachers be differentiated, ordered hierarchically,

and allocated on the basis of professional competence. (p. 168)

Other authors argue basically from the same premise (Bailey, 1991; Cohee, 1991; Keith & Girling, 1991).

Keith and Girling suggest a new concept called "policy trust agreements," which expand teacher involvement and responsibilities. They have adapted work from Mitchell (1986).

All of these moves point toward a much more positive view of unions, collective negotiations, and teacher and administrator professionalism. We can no longer be at odds with each other and split our ranks. All educators must respond collaboratively to the external pressures of reform. We can increase professionalism through empowerment.

What are the steps toward change?

1. Boards, administrators, and teacher representatives must sit down in a problem-solving mode and discuss the relative gains and positive outcomes of previous contract negotiations.
2. Using a representative task force and an external consultant, a problem-solving and trust agreement plan must be drawn up and approved by all concerned.
3. The new plan must be implemented and judged with predetermined criteria so that adjustments can be made for future betterment of the field of education.

Review of Key Concepts

❑ Power is the only thing that multiplies when it is divided.
❑ Using teachers as school and classroom researchers and data collectors is one way to empower.
❑ Differentiated empowerment, which provides specialty roles within the teacher ranks, is a workable empowerment application.
❑ Professional teachers and administrators must learn to police themselves as other professional groups have done.
❑ The adversarial conflict between teacher unions and management must shift to the creation of policy trust agreements.

References

Bailey, W. J. (1991). *School-site management applied.* Lancaster, PA: Technomic.

Cohee, W. (1991). *An analysis of negotiations* (Executive Position Paper). Newark: University of Delaware.

Edelfelt, R. (1985). Career ladders: Then and now. *Educational Leadership, 43*(3), 62-66.

Hall, R. H. (1975). *Occupations and the social structure.* Englewood Cliffs, NJ: Prentice-Hall.

Keith, S., & Girling, R. (1991). *Education, management and participation.* Boston: Allyn & Bacon.

Mitchell, D. (1986, September). Policy trust agreements: A better approach to school labor relations. *Thrust, 11,* 11-14.

Shedd, J., & Bacharach, S. (1991). *Tangled hierarchies.* San Francisco: Jossey-Bass.

Shulman, L. (1991, April). *Teacher improvement.* Speech presented to North Carolina State University, Raleigh.

5

How to Improve Student Learning

5.1 What Are Recent Innovations in the Subject Areas?

William Johnson (1989, p. 245) states:

> Universities did not lead an intellectual revolution which transformed the training of teachers. The experience in education is better described as a series of local uprisings each decade or so which have had little enduring impact except, perhaps, to clutter the curricular landscape with dead or wounded programs and theories.

Thus, in a few short words, Johnson sadly describes the state of the art in curriculum and instruction in pessimistic and, many would agree, accurate words. There are continual innovations in the subject areas. There will always be innovations, but how do we avoid the dead and wounded?

The answer to orienting an organization to be open to change and innovation and at the same time minimizing the age-old problems of pendulum swings and dying programs is simple: We must restructure and empower if we are going to develop lasting systems for discovering, implementing, and evaluating educational programs. I will outline innovations in selected subject areas that hold promise for the twenty-first century, including a separate section on technology. This is risky because it might reinforce Johnson's claim. The most important question is this: How does an educational system deal with such innovations? So, as you read through one author's opinion of what looks new, think more about how your district would approach implementation and evaluation. Local schools with empowered teachers have the best opportunity to avoid trendy curriculums, or least they have the best chance of adopting, modifying, and integrating new material.

The following are examples of subject matter innovations.

A. *Social Studies*

"Social Studies is the study of how citizens in a society make personal and public decisions on issues that affect their destiny" (Cleveland, 1985). Thus social studies programs need to rely on teaching students to recognize, analyze, and act on problems or decisions that affect an individual's, a group's, and a nation's well-being (Bragaw & Hartoonian, 1988). With these assumptions, instructional programs in social studies take on a clear but probably markedly different mode than traditional methods. It implies that social studies experiences must prepare students to be knowledgeable, active citizens. It implies instructional strategies of field studies, role-playing, current events, integration of social studies with other subjects, core curriculums, information use, legal concerns, problem solving, decision making, communication, values clarification as well as scanning newspapers for public policy issues and other techniques of relevance. The importance of relevance in the curriculum is not new to the literature, but did it really strike home in many classrooms? All of these kinds of instructional strategies need be grounded in the subject matter content of geography, history, and government, but the evaluation of this "new" curriculum must come from an experience base. You do not teach relevance and test rote memory. Integrating content with process and relevance is the challenge to social studies teachers in the future. I submit that this cannot be worked out at the district or state levels. How will your district or school deal with this challenge?

B. Science

One of the age-old curricular arguments in the science education field tries to solve the secondary science problem of teaching all children the importance of science in our daily lives, a respect for ecology, and a technological preparation for everyone. At the same time, high schools must prepare college-bound students with advanced laboratory science courses. It is difficult to break away from the traditional sequence of biology-chemistry-physics.

One solution is to provide academic science courses that prepare students for expected needs in college and to be potential scientists as well as to require that all students be "grounded" in the basic sciences if they choose not to take the academic path. These latter students would take the applied/technical path, which provides students an opportunity to gain general knowledge in the major sciences (chemistry, physics, biology, earth science) while stressing the application of science to everyday problems and the world of work. This is not a new idea, but it is hardly ever carried out for more than one general science course. We are facing a world of ever-increasing technology and scientific advances. Should we not educate *all* children in these basic science groups? For years, even college-bound students not interested in science have elected biology and perhaps chemistry; but, because they believe science gets harder as the years go by, they skip physics. Is a student educated if he or she has not had any physics since grade school? I think not.

Well, here is a practical idea: High schools should require all students to take earth science, biology, chemistry, and physics. To accommodate learning levels and interest, choices are made by the students each year as to the degree of in-depth study (applied/technical or college bound). If one can avoid the pitfalls of tracking, why not try this in your high schools? How would you go about it? Could the problem be handled differently in different high schools within the same district?

c. Mathematics

Every state in the union has made efforts in the 1980s and 1990s to enhance the mathematics education of all students. The experts in mathematics education emphasize that programs of the future must include computational skills *and* concept development. These future programs must teach problem-solving skills and must relate mathematics to advancing technology. Practicing administrators and math teachers face the practical problems of math programs including issues such as the role computers and calculators should play in daily instruction. Instructional techniques seem to play an unusually large part when examining the math curriculum. What is the best way to teach math at each level? I think the techniques and the conceptual problems of math education have been dealt with satisfactorily in the literature. The basic problem with math education comes down to implementing new programs, schedules, requirements, and evaluations of learning. Are these problems best solved at the school building level?

Allow me to provide an example of an exemplary secondary math program that was developed by the math department of Concord High School in Wilmington, Delaware, some 20 years ago (Bailey, 1974). The math department, along with the school's curriculum council, the principal, and the district office as a support service, decided that all students need geometry and algebra to function in a modern world. Therefore all students were required to take algebra and geometry regardless of previous math records. The problem was not philosophical—it was logistical. We arranged a continuous-progress, nongraded math curriculum that block scheduled groups of students in large team-taught sections that accommodated varying learning groups based on their progress through the math courses. As a result of this flexibility, some students finished algebra 1 before spring break and some students took two years, but every student learned algebra. This concept is based on ample evidence that most students can learn most subjects if time is not a factor. Student evaluation was based on a credit or no-credit basis. You could not flunk math but you might not get credit unless you mastered a topic (i.e., geometry). Advanced students took calculus and so on in a more traditional format. Thus we solved the problem of meeting the needs of society (everyone needs algebra and geometry to function effectively) and the needs of individual students at the same time. It was a lot of work for faculty, but the program worked. Mind you, this was 20 years ago. What happens to innovations such as this? Most high schools in the country today still arrange math instruction the same way it was done in the 1940s and 1950s. With the capacity of computers to track individual student progress, there is no excuse for high schools not to revise their programs to meet the needs of individuals.

It is not possible for a state or a large school district to work out the details of this sample program. It can and must be done at the local school building level. A system of schools that empowers teachers can manage innovative programs such as the one described. How does your system plan to improve your math program?

D. Language Arts Instruction

Stop and think about all the research and theory that have been generated regarding reading, writing, and literature studies. All states have recommended programs of studies; most colleges of education have faculty experts in language arts; every district has a program of studies for English; and research articles in this area are plentiful. We know how students cognitively acquire a knowledge base in language. We have national, professional organizations built upon interests in teaching English;

the government has supplied millions of dollars for research and development projects in language arts; and the list of achievements goes on. And, after all of this academic hoopla, Johnny still cannot read or write.

At least the national reports are filled with evidence that many students are not learning to read or write adequately and seemingly only the best students appreciate the study of literature. We have increasing national dropout rates, lower SAT scores, and increasing illiteracy.

At the risk of being simplistic and offending all of my language arts professor colleagues, I believe we have forgotten the child in the learning process. Authors such as Keefe (1989) have argued for personalizing education, but no one seems to be listening. Keefe states that schools are not organized for personalization, they are geared to crowds. Numbers, groups, scheduling problems, grade levels, test scores, and the latest cognitive research are not geared toward the individual student with his or her unique learning style.

In an interesting empirical study dealing with specific writing instruction strategies, Englert, Raphael, Anderson, Anthony, and Stevens (1991, p. 337) report: "The results support the importance of instruction that makes the writing processes and strategies visible to students through teacher-student and student-student dialogues." The authors conclude by saying that "the writing process need not be decomposed or reduced to a sequential set of strategies that are learned in isolation" (p. 368). With the proper degree of teacher dialogue (I interpret this to mean paying attention to individual student needs and learning styles), the writing process can be enhanced.

If your English teachers wanted to restructure the writing and reading experience in their individual schools to accommodate the need to personalize the language arts instruction, would they be allowed to? Does the autonomy exist to encourage professionals to innovate instruction for the twenty-first century? How does your school organization handle improvements in language arts? Does the change process enhance teacher empowerment or discourage it? "Turned-on" teachers willing to personalize language arts instruction can make a difference—

a difference that is not being made with our grand research and
development projects and statewide curriculum guides.

Of course, each school must make decisions about the total
curriculum, including subjects such as technology education,
physical and health education, and the arts. The same questions
of discovering, selecting, implementing, and evaluating apply to
all curricular decisions. A restructured system of schools is
smaller and leaner and, consequently, better able to make on-
site decisions that are proper for the individual school. The leading schools of the future will be those that have restructured
their curriculum to encompass things such as integrating subject
areas, greater student-teacher interaction, lectures used less
but more purposefully, emphasis on relevance and applied
knowledge, heterogeneous classes, flexible teaching groups,
flexible scheduling, collaboration among teachers, and community support. Will your school be a leader in restructuring curriculum or will it only point to programs that died or were
wounded?

5.2 What Are the Time Wasters?

Schools should be considered workplaces. Students' studies
are their work. Teachers' work is guiding those students. Productivity in a workplace is directly related to time management.
One way for school decision makers to increase productivity is
to restructure the organization so that time is not wasted. If
schools can improve the use of time, school workers can improve
student learning. Are there time wasters in your school? Let's
look at some examples.

Most readers should be familiar with the studies classified as
"student engaged time" or "time on task." The results are clear.
If a faculty can increase the amount of available time that is
spent in direct learning activities, they can increase student
achievement. So the first step an empowered school needs to
make as they study time management is to analyze the classroom. Comparing the time that is spent on reading announcements, administrative matters, collecting milk money, gazing

out the window, or waiting for the bell to ring with the time that is spent providing instruction and real learning activities is vital. These studies can be conducted by the faculty in a collegial setting where the climate is conducive to adult learning. As a result, teachers may want to restructure their classroom time.

The next item of time to consider is the school day. As in the classroom, noninstructional time is important to consider. Analyze recess, lunchtime, homerooms, hall passing time, assemblies, waiting for busses, teacher planning time, special classes (e.g., art), parent days, holiday special events (e.g., Halloween), birthday parties, waiting to be seen by the principal, committee meetings, faculty meetings, fire drills, "dress up" and "dress down" days, snow days, and so on. I am not saying all of these have to be eliminated. I am saying they all have to be studied on a regular basis in the context of how they contribute to the main function of this workplace: learning.

For example, a prime consideration of a restructured school should be a concern about school climate. Perhaps some of the above activities contribute to a positive school climate. If so, do you have evidence? Ministudies can be conducted to learn the true value of any of these activities and if in fact they help this particular school meet its goals. Perhaps recess is too short. Perhaps the school should have more assemblies or more hall passing time. A restructured school looks at effectiveness and does not continue activities, habits, traditions, schedules, and time frames because they are efficient (or because people are lazy, in terms of using last year's plans). Can your school(s) improve student learning by looking at the use of the school day?

The third area concerned with time is the school year. Of course, much of the school year is dictated by most state's regulations. These regulations can be changed and schools can maximize the time provided. For the purposes of this section, let's look at some of the school year options. They need restructuring as well.

The time allocated by most states for student days compared with teacher days is interesting. The typical requirement is 180 days for students and another 5 days for teachers. Schools that restructure to improve learning need to look at the ratio of teacher planning time and student attendance time. Empowered schools require that teachers plan and develop collectively. Five days a year does not suffice.

Can you imagine a school faculty deciding on how many days they need for planning in any given year? Assuming there will be few extra dollars to pay teachers, the time would have to come from student attendance days. Only a school faculty can determine how many days they need. Additional and effective planning time could increase student learning more than any other single national report's recommendation. Other professionals and other organizations spend considerable time in professional development and planning. Empowering teachers without increasing professional time does not make sense. Finding more time for teachers to interact does make sense.

The other major consideration is the time in school compared with the yearly calendar. A sprinkling of schools around the country have experimented with "year-round schools." It is difficult to gather information regarding the success of these schools and generalize from it. It is feasible to experiment on a local basis and, through various forms of action research, determine whether these plans are profitable. It makes sense to disperse the learning time to students in shorter and more frequent time slots, but, of course, there are many political considerations.

5.3 Scheduling for Student Learning

Basically, principals can schedule for student learning or they can schedule for various adult needs. Adult needs include the ease of scheduling in the same way we did last year, satisfying teacher needs, saving money on computerized scheduling (the master schedule came this way from the computer service), scheduling different buildings the same to share teachers, accommodating the supervisor of lunch programs, or simple limits of creativity. The above reasons may be very efficient; but, because we are searching for effectiveness, let's look at some better ways to schedule for student learning.

The basic rule of scheduling is that form must follow function. The general steps are, first, to decide what the needs of students are. Then, second, how can faculty be arranged to best accommodate those needs? Third, what are the limitations of rooms and facilities and equipment? When those steps are completed, the best form of scheduling can be determined.

Taking a fresh look at scheduling may cause a restructuring of the scheduling process. The structure of the learning experiences must be flexible enough to allow for different sized groups to serve the different functions of instruction. Teachers must feel they have the freedom to structure their own activities for their specific objectives. Structured learning experiences can occur in four basic grouping arrangements.

Individuals. Individuals are involved in instruction in independent study (assignment of independent work for a prescribed length of time); individual study course (primarily applicable to advanced senior high students who study a complete course on an individual basis with supervision from a member of the faculty); teacher conferencing (the research on dialoguing shows that flexibility in the schedule can free teachers to do more tutoring); unscheduled time (if one of the school's goals is to train students to be independent learners, then perhaps students need unscheduled time to follow their pursuits).

Small groups. The small group, properly coached, can be a very effective scheduling device for learning. The purposes could include discussion groups, study groups, work-alike groups (e.g., students who are all having trouble with improper fractions), cooperative learning groups, team competition, reading groups, laboratory/field study groups, or project groups. From kindergarten to graduate school, the small group is a viable learning option. The size of the group obviously depends upon the function, but a general guideline is from 3 or 4 students to a maximum of 15. The important point is that the basic schedule can allow for this kind of flexibility. If teachers cannot schedule small groups within the basic schedule, then the master schedule is not serving the learning needs of students.

Classroom groups. The standard classroom is a group. For most subjects and for many purposes of an instructional unit, the classroom is *not* the right size group. The class-size group is overused because it serves the adult needs of efficiency. It is a lot of trouble in some schools to change the schedule to accommodate different functions.

Standard classroom numbers might vary from 20 to 40 students depending on the purpose. For example, a high school typing class, training students for the keyboard, might use a 40-student class if the facilities allow, while an elementary group of students studying science might be better off with 20 students. The classroom group works well for meetings, basic instruction, organizational activities, testing, art, music, physical education, or advanced single sections in high schools (such as German 4). Restructured schools must analyze their needs and schedule classroom size groupings prudently.

Large groups. Large groups can be scheduled in special areas. Physical requirements such as visibility, audibility, and seating are the only restrictions. The number of students can be from 50 to 200 or 300. It is not the size of the audience that defines the activity, it is the purpose that should dictate it. Of course, every day in traditional schools, large group lectures are inappropriately given to 20 students. Proper presentations might include lectures, movies, demonstrations, panel discussions with audience, debates, guest speakers, testing (carefully), organization- and procedure-oriented meetings, or motivational meetings. Does your master schedule allow for large group instruction?

The recommendation to assign all teachers to work teams was made earlier. When discussing scheduling, however, the question of team teaching should be considered because team teaching is another way to build flexibility into the schedule. *Team teaching* has many definitions but it is used here to imply jointly teaching or sharing learning experiences with the same group of students. In Table 5.1, Bailey (1974) outlines some questions and considerations about team teaching that are applicable to this discussion.

If there are no existing examples of either teaming or variable grouping in a building, there are several procedures that can be initiated that will lead to experimentation on a minor scale and possible transition to more complicated plans involving the total school:

• Visit schools where teaming is working.
• The self-contained teacher can group students within his or her class for special projects. By varying the kinds and functions of the group, the teacher can begin to evaluate the process. These groups can meet in the class or in the hallway.
• Two teachers, after having experienced the second suggestion above, can combine their groups for the same activities.
• Two or more teachers can combine classes for large group activities, such as lectures or movies.
• Several teachers can plan a unit together and report back to each other regarding the outcomes.
• A teacher can be very explicit about his or her teaching so that the activities are clearly labeled: lecture, discussion, independent study. Without these demarcations, there is a common tendency to have continuous recitation activities with no particular instructional strategy.
• Several teachers can swap classes for a week during the year for variety or to capitalize on specialties.
• The better students in a class can be put on a several-week independent study project.
• The slowest student in the class can be given special assignments and tests.
• Students can be allowed to retake a test at least once as they become individually ready for it.
• For the teacher to engage in quality discussion with a small group, he or she can work with half the class at a time. The other half can be given an assignment and can go to the library, study hall, another teacher's class, or an empty room. Then reverse the process.
• The schedule can be built to accommodate these possibilities. For example, schedule at least two classes of U.S. history in adjoining rooms during the same period. (pp. 149-151)

The important point about scheduling is that the master schedule must be arranged to allow for flexibility because

TABLE 5.1 Teaming Variables and Their Influences

Variables	(+) Positive Influences	(−) Negative Influences
Professionalism	Teacher-peer evaluation Ineffective teachers improve Better staff utilization Increase in teacher enthusiasm	Threatening to some teachers The very best teachers may regress toward the mean Overspecialization might upset negotiations
Administration	Better instruction for the administrative involvement	Possible increased costs Administrative interference Complications to scheduling process
Instructional strategies	Individualization Variety of instructors Curricular improvements	Impersonal for students Confusing for students Parent misunderstandings
Logistics	Number of students and teachers may be conducive to teaming Block scheduling may open up student options	Number of students and number of sections may not be enough for good teaming situations
Planning	Results in better instruction "Two heads are better than one" Ideas are shared	Finding time for planning and in-service can be a real problem Lesson planning gets complicated and emotional
Facilities	Increase in creativity Existing facilities usually adaptable Better utilization and efficiency Daily decision for flexibility	Securing certain areas could be a problem Facilities may dictate instructional strategies Possible costs for renovations

TABLE 5.1 (continued)

Variables	(+) Positive Influences	(−) Negative Influences
Articulation	Meeting of objectives is facilitated "Group think" Better sequencing Greater consistency	Restricting academic freedom Some rigidity in structures and procedures is necessary Bureaucracy
Leadership	Staff development opportunities Rewards master teachers	Internal fighting for control "We have arrived" syndrome may inhibit future changes
Socialization	Teachers get to know a few peers really well Process of decision making good for personal growth experiences	Teachers become isolated in teams and departments
Evaluation	Becomes more objective and more consistent department Requires introspection and vulnerability, which should result in course improvements	May bring about some undue pressures Rigidity "creeps in" Exposure of evaluation controversies may become an "issue" for whole school

SOURCE: Bailey (1974, p. 150).

learning needs vary from week to week. With the advent of computers, scheduling variations should be easy. If your high school has six periods a day with every subject given 52 minutes, if your middle school is scheduled like a junior high school, and if your elementary school is scheduled only with self-contained classrooms, it is time to restructure the schedule based on some of the principles discussed above.

An example of a flexible scheduling mode is some form of block scheduling. Block scheduling can be used at any grade level and allows teachers to decide on a weekly basis the most appropriate schedule for learning. There will always be time and space limitations—that is the definition of a schedule—but assigning large blocks of time to several teachers or teams may be one solution for your school.

5.4 Beware of Sacred Cows!

Schools are organizations, and organizations develop organizational histories, which have a great tendency to become institutionalized. Once a rule, practice, procedure, or policy becomes institutionalized, it can very easily become a "sacred cow." A sacred cow in this case is defined as an idea that has outlived its usefulness but remains because of tradition and needs to be reexamined. The sacred cow becomes part of the organizational history and thus is difficult to remove partly because there is security associated with the expected and predictable. The sacred cow syndrome is not to be confused with school identity traditions that may serve a useful purpose. What are some typical sacred cows associated with curriculum and instruction and student learning?

- High schools:
    seven-period days
    50-minute periods
    homerooms
    three-period lunches
    lectures as the prime instructional strategy
    honor roles
    textbook-dominated courses
    teaching to the tests
    algebra 2 before geometry (or was it the other way around?)
    memorization and rote learning as the main pedagogy
    restrictions regarding the library
    hall passes

       no schedule changes after the second week of school
       no schedule changes based on the student's dislike of
         the teacher
       U.S. history in the 11th grade
       requiring only one year of science
       requiring only one year of math
       isolated, self-contained classes

- Middle schools:
       ability grouping
       high school-type schedules
       interscholastic sports
       academic departmentalization
       high school-type socialization patterns
       inflexible schedules
       self-contained classes
       stressful climates
       emphasis on grades, tests, and IQ scores
       bells

- Elementary schools:
       ability grouping
       bells
       seat work
       report cards with letter grades
       student desks in rows
       grade retention
       failures
       principals with high school background
       once-a-week physical education
       spankings
       same textbook for all
       didactic pedagogy
       boring classrooms

If you don't like my examples, create your own. Perhaps a task force of teachers and an external consultant using devices such as curriculum audit or organizational analysis procedures could systematically examine current practices dealing with structures that affect learning. A large part of restructuring is self-examination. The greatest need for self-examination is in the instructional delivery system of each school. Improving student learning is a constant challenge.

5.5 A Few Notes About Technology

One cannot even consider restructuring student learning without recognizing the place of technology. There are many resources for educational technology and a few are listed at the end of this section. The purpose of this book is not to delve into extensive futuristic devices that might cause a revolution in student learning but simply to mention some practical innovations that are available. The intent is to cause curriculum and instruction practitioners to *observe* what is available, *analyze* what can be useful locally, and *prescribe* what can be implemented.

> We do not believe the educational system needs repairing: We believe it must be rebuilt. . . . The focus of schooling must shift from teaching to learning, from the passive acquisition of facts and routines to the active application of ideas to problems. That transition makes the role of the teacher more important, not less . . . video recorders and laser disks players are now available that can bring large amounts of information to individual students on demand, including high quality visual images. . . . The prospects are fascinating. These technologies should make it possible to relieve teachers of much of the burden of imparting information to students, thereby freeing them for coaching, diagnosing learning difficulties, developing students' creative and problem-solving capabilities and participating in school management. (*A Nation Prepared: Teachers for the 21st Century,* 1986)

We need to fundamentally rethink what we are doing and how we are doing it—to avoid the obvious in technology is cheating taxpayers.

Empowered schools need to establish decision procedures to grapple with the use, cost, and evaluation of technology, such as the following:

- computers—administrative and general classroom use
- specific computer-based instruction models
- "expert system" data bases

- calculators
- word processors
- telecommunication
- CAD (computer-assisted drafting)
- distance and satellite learning
- videodisc instruction
- technology education (replaces industrial arts)
- robotics
- digital video interactives
- idea processors
- artificial intelligence computers (diagnosing learning styles)
- national data base linkages
- desktop publishing
- commercial videos
- video recorders
- cable television
- computerized IEPs (individual education plans)
- requirement of faculty computer literacy-
- computer programming skills
- CD-ROM (compact disc-read-only memory)

This list is neither complete nor in priority order; that is the job of each individual school. Once the faculty has an understanding of the options and costs, a decision process can be used to set local priorities. If a list such as the one above is used, a simple priority ranking can be generated by using the nominal method. Every one of the decision makers (a committee or the entire faculty) rank orders the list and the totals are summarized (a low total is high priority and so on).

The most difficult job of the technology change agent is to assist teachers in the assimilation and enculturation of the technology into their mainstream behaviors. Collins and Martinez (1989) have good suggestions regarding computer use. Their recommended steps are as follows:

1. Evaluate the content of computer studies in your school district (school).
2. Provide in-service training to all teachers.
3. Encourage classroom teachers to use computers within their own subject areas.

4. Sensitize teachers and administrators to equity issues in computer education.

An interesting relationship between computers and effective instruction comes from Larkin and Chabay (1989). They recommend the following features of effective instruction that apply to computer-based instruction:

1. Develop a detailed description of the processes the student needs to acquire.
2. Systematically address all knowledge included in the description of the process.
3. Let most instruction occur through active work on tasks.
4. Give feedback on specific tasks as soon as possible after an error has been made.
5. Once is not enough. Let students encounter each knowledge unit several times.
6. Limit demands on student attention.

Clearly, we have a lot to learn. The old teaching methods will not work any longer. We must restructure to significantly improve instruction and learning. The technology is here. It is *not* something of the future that future faculties will have to handle. If there ever was an application of the expression "the future is now," this is it. Prepare accordingly. This task is too large for a state or a district to engage in effectively. Ironically, we must personalize and humanize the move toward technology by implementation generated at the local school level.

5.6 Selected Resources for Technology and Instruction and Learning

Association for Supervision and Curriculum Development (Alexandria, VA). (1991, May). *Educational Leadership, 48*(8).
Cetron, M. (1985). *Schools of the future.* New York: McGraw-Hill.

Collins, B. (1985). Reflections on inequities in computer education: Do the rich get richer? *Education and Computing, 1,* 179-186.

Klopher, L. (1986, November). The coming generation of computing software. *The Science Teacher,* pp. 33-36.

Litchfield, B. (1990, September). Slipping a disk in the classroom: The latest in video technology. *Science and Children,* pp. 16-31.

Martinez, M. E., & Mead, N. A. (1988). *Computer competence: The first national assessment.* Princeton, NJ: Educational Testing Service.

Resnick, L., & Klopfer, L. (Eds.). (1989). *Toward the thinking curriculum: Current cognitive research, ASCD yearbook.* Alexandria, VA: Association for Supervision and Curriculum Development (ASCD).

Sununu, J. H. (1987). Will technologies make learning and teaching easier? *Phi Delta Kappan, 68,* 220-222.

Review of Key Concepts

❏ The whole purpose of restructuring is to improve student learning.

❏ There will always be new ideas about teaching and learning in the separate subject areas. Each school must consider how they will adopt and adapt these innovations as they surface.

❏ All aspects of the use of time (daily, weekly, monthly, and yearly) must be analyzed on a regular basis to ascertain whether time is being wasted—because restructured, effective schools use time wisely.

❏ There are many sacred cows to watch out for when restructuring. Some of these are self-contained classrooms, standard period days, standard-length class periods, ability groups, letter grades, grade retention, and student desks in rows.

❏ An important component of restructuring is maximizing the technology that is available to us.

References

A nation prepared: Teachers for the 21st century. (1986). Princeton, NJ: Carnegie Forum.

Bailey, W. J. (1974). *Managing self-renewal in secondary education.* Englewood Cliffs, NJ: Educational Technology.

Bragaw, D., & Hartoonian, M. (1988). Social studies: The study of people in society. In R. Brandt (Ed.), *Content of the curriculum.* Alexandria, VA: Association for Supervision and Curriculum Development (ASCD).

Cleveland, H. (1985). *The knowledge executive.* New York: Harper & Row.

Collins, B., & Martinez, M. (1989). Computers in U.S. and Canadian schools: Have we made progress? *NASSP Bulletin, 73,* 5-9.

Englert, C., Raphael, T., Anderson, L., Anthony, H., & Stevens, D. (1991). Making strategies and self talk visible: Writing instruction in regular and special education classrooms. *American Educational Research Journal, 28,* 337-372.

Johnson, W. (1989). Teachers and teacher training in the twentieth century. In D. Warren (Ed.), *American teachers: Histories of a profession at work.* New York: Macmillan.

Keefe, J. W. (1989). Personalized education. In H. Walberg & J. Lane (Eds.), *Organizing for learning: Toward the 21st century.* Reston, VA: National Association of Secondary Principals.

Larkin, J., & Chabay, R. (1989). Research in teaching scientific thinking: Implications for computer-based instruction. *Toward the thinking curriculum: Current cognitive research, ASCD yearbook* (pp. 150-172). Alexandria, VA: ASCD.

6

Strategies for Change

6.1 Viewing Leaders as Change Agents

While consulting with a large rural school district recently, I had the opportunity to observe the importance of administrative leadership. The scene was a retreat workshop for administrators and the topic was school site management. As a consultant and workshop leader, I led the group through the rationale for restructuring and empowerment. After this broad and conceptual view, the expected questions from the group concerned the practical implications for their district. Their real questions were these: "As a district, are we really serious about school site management?" and "What are the parameters?" These important questions must be answered by the superintendent, who is the social architect for the organization.

So the superintendent addressed some 50 administrators and attempted to reassure them that changes were forthcoming and also describe some of the parameters. And here is the challenge of leadership! It was obvious to me that, as a group, they were *not* convinced. The lack of acceptance of the new ideas and the subtle mistrust of the superintendent can be explained in cultural terms. Schools and school districts have assimilated a social order. They exhibit subcultural behaviors as part of that social order. District personnel accumulate beliefs about students, curriculum, governance, and administrator roles. For example, teachers and administrators in the above district have learned to associate the superintendent's role with the previous messages he has passed on to them. Those messages, which after a few years have been acculturated, sound like the following: "We must follow state guidelines." "If the school board will let us." "We need to watch the budget." "We need to standardize administrative procedures." "Let's develop a common discipline code." "We must give the parents the same message." "We can get in trouble if we don't follow directions from the department of public instruction." "I would like to raise the district test scores." "Don't worry, if I don't get after you, you know you are doing a good job." Or, "We need team players." These are the messages of efficiency, conformity, correct practices, and social order.

For the superintendent, changing his message from the importance of order to the importance of change, creativity, and decentralized governance is going to be very difficult. The superintendent and all of his predecessors have been too "successful." A significant organizational change, such as school site management, requires a substantive change in the organizational culture. Restructuring asks for a change in the social order. Because "leadership" gave us the previous order, leadership must give us the new order. But this is a gigantic shift of paradigms, which many superintendents do not appreciate.

If leaders were viewed as change agents, then a message of change would be easier. If leaders are viewed as keepers of the old order, then change is very difficult. Change strategies of this magnitude must deal with the culture of the district and the ethos of each school. What kind of climate has been established by administrative leadership? The research is clear about the importance of leadership to an educational institution: It is crucial to effectiveness. School people just have to think differently about the impact they are having.

Educational institutions need administrators who view themselves and are viewed by teachers as change agents. There is an amazing need on the part of most teachers to conform to the norm. If the norm is conservative, the behavior will be conservative and difficult to change. If the norm is more progressive, change will be easier. *It is the role of leadership to enhance the climate of the schools by preparing them for change.* Thus leaders, by definition, must be change agents.

Change is more than an intellectual exercise. Change is systemic and it challenges leadership. Educational leaders of the twenty-first century must lead teachers from correct practice to successful practice, from a concentration on service to a focus on learning, and from "red tape" to personalization of schooling. Administrators must go from being carriers of policy to being change agents.

What can administrators do to change their image as part of conducting a district toward restructuring?

1. Explain the reasoning behind the traditional approach to administration as implementors of policy.
2. Explain the need for changes in governance, policy, and culture.
3. Start a pilot project that will be successful and illustrate the new order of things.
4. Obtain board approval for the changes and create a focus of energies toward the new targets.
5. Talk with administrators and teachers to demonstrate an understanding of the difficulty of change in social order but, at the same time, do not back off from the long-range goals.
6. Whenever possible, hire new district leaders who exhibit change agent skills and creative mind-sets.
7. Hire consultants who can receive some of the complaints and "take some of the heat" associated with restructuring.

8. Repeat the change message like a broken record.
9. Be patient with people and their struggle for change but keep the ideas in front of everyone as a constant reminder that "we are serious."
10. Use data survey feedback to assess the climate for change.
11. Evaluate outcomes periodically and disseminate information on outcomes.

6.2 Using a Change Matrix

In addition to an understanding and appreciation for the importance of culture in the change process, the change agent needs a plan. This change agent can be the superintendent or an assistant superintendent or a long-term consultant or a task force leader. Because change involving restructuring is quite complex, recognition of the variables of successful planned change is important. The matrix below should help the change agent coordinate these variables. There are two major indices. The first is the *change process,* which involves variables such as

- a *readiness* to change that in large part is grounded in the cultural components described in the preceding section;
- *planning,* that is, someone and/or some group must have a plan that can be reviewed and evaluated by all interested parties;
- the *implementation phase*, which needs to be monitored carefully in terms of factors affecting morale, motivation, public relations, and general effectiveness; and
- an *evaluation* of the complete change process as well as intermediate sources of feedback from those affected by the change.

The other index comprises the *components of successful planned change* that have been gleaned from the research literature:

- *Leadership* is required in change efforts.
- *Adaptability* (or the ability to adapt) is necessary (because nothing comes in its pure form).

Variables of the Change Process	Components of Successful Planned Change					
	Leadership	Adaptability	Training and Development	Work group cooperation	Conflict management	Support groups
Readiness						
Planning						
Implementation						
Evaluation						

Figure 6.1. Organizational Change Matrix

- *Training and development* are necessary for all parties concerned (in the case of restructuring, it is essential that the school board also receive training).
- *Work group cooperation* is required. Earlier in the book, a description of work groups and their usefulness to productivity were addressed. Organizations must employ work groups within the organization as the basic change unit.
- *Conflict management* should be part of training because restructuring will feed conflict. It must be remembered that conflict is not "bad" but simply a normal human reaction to stress.
- *Support groups* organized by the change agent to provide early acceptance and to influence others are a crucial component of any change strategy.

Frequently reviewing and evaluating these components and variables is an excellent way to integrate them into a complete planning picture. The resulting matrix as an analytical tool is presented in Figure 6.1.

For each cell in the matrix, there are checkpoints to consider. For example, *leadership* needs to possess at least a minimal degree of readiness; leaders must plan, be able to administer the implementation, and be responsible for an evaluation scheme prior to the change. The *adaptability* factor affects everyone in that evaluation schemes may have to be adapted, implementation never goes exactly as planned, and the planning process itself must be flexible. There are readiness factors, planning needs, implementation problems, and evaluation requirements for all *training and development.* There will be *conflict* in all variables, and so on. The other cells are as applicable.

Another factor in successful planned change is the degree or extensiveness question. Just how far do the decision makers want to go with restructuring? Do the decision makers want complete transformation that refutes standardization, central control, and externally imposed rules? Do they want to embrace policy changes, establish a climate for problem solving and inquiry, use building or work group autonomy? Should teacher empowerment be equal to that of university professors? How about decentralization of the budget?

Perhaps the decision makers are content with what might be called "realignment," which is making alignment shifts where one can, decentralizing decision making without completely restructuring the table of organization, and improving the working conditions and prestige of teachers.

A much lesser degree of change might include labeling what some of the principals have been doing anyway, adopting a rhetoric of change, and making the most of de facto diversity because conformity to school-based management is difficult to achieve.

The latter option is easier to achieve and is more comfortable for most parties because it does not create a lot of conflict. The more complete the transformation, as in the first case in the previous chapter, the more dramatic the change and the more risky it is. Proper involvement of all parties in this kind of in-depth restructuring can be a powerful agent for successful restructuring.

Just as this book advocates increased participation in decision making, a change agent needs to use high-involvement management. The change process itself must be replete with shared decision making and ample time for discussion. Anticipated group responses to the changes, evaluation of training workshops, and planning groups for the strategic changes are important.

A poor example of this concept occurred at a school district workshop to install school site management. Several days of in-service were set aside for the training, but all of the training sessions were designed by the assistant superintendent and the consultant. How can we train people in participatory procedures without getting input from participants for the training? What irony do you create?

Still another device for successful change that needs to be covered briefly is the time line and schedule for implementation. The change agent can use the change matrix as provided and fill in the boxes with anticipated completion/achievement dates. There are simple time lines and other management devices to plan and monitor implementation but dates do not have to be rigid. Without some target dates, however, it is much too easy to loose momentum. This loss of momentum, and deterrents created by critics (who are always there), will cause the project to fail.

The final test of effective change leadership requires the change agent to do some soul-searching as to his or her own motivations. Personal bias, past experiences, positive and negative events of the past, personal values, and personality all play a part in our behavior. What are the true motivations for creating this fuss about schooling? If they are purely personal, there may be better expenditures of time and energy. If they cause organizational improvements, the results are worthy of the effort.

Finally, Hersey and Blanchard (1988) offer three competencies of leadership that are applicable to the change agent. They are (a) diagnosing, being able to understand the situation you are trying to influence; (b) adapting, being able to adapt leadership behavior to meet the contingencies of the situation; and (c) communicating, being able to communicate in a manner that people can understand and accept. Good change agents diagnose, adapt, and communicate. Restructuring will tax these skills as no other change project. Prepare accordingly.

6.3 Establishing a Task Force

Establishing a task force (or some other appropriate participatory vehicle) is an extremely important step in the change process. The main reasons for an auxiliary administrative body are (a) that change agents need to practice what they preach about participation and (b) that the current governance and decision-making system is probably not capable of planning itself out of business—which is why we need to restructure in the first place.

Thinking that a centralized system can restructure itself without outside help, strong internal change agent leadership, and some kind of ad hoc task force that can operate extra systemically is somewhat like asking disadvantaged people to pick themselves up by their own bootstraps. If the current mechanisms were capable of restructuring, those mechanisms would have started up long before, as soon as it became clear that schools need changing.

The answer then is for the superintendent to form a district committee, team, or task force. He or she should give them considerable time, money, and authority and use their recommendations—unless they are illegal or immoral. This task force must have high prestige, be composed of influential leaders, and be composed of sensitive as well as intelligent people. Runkel, Schmuck, Arends, and Francis (1978) provide guidelines for selecting task force members:

1. Look for participants with time and energy who are willing to discuss their problems and the problems of the school.
2. Look for administrators who realize that short-term projects of the past are not bearing fruit and who are ready to plan at least a year in advance.
3. Look for teachers who have not as yet succumbed to pessimism.
4. Look for those who can be motivated by a vision of joint achievement, by a vision of greater control over their own work, and by the yearning for camaraderie.

5. Look for those who understand that schools are complex systems and that norms in work groups are the key to productivity and change.
6. Look for those who have faith that there must be a better way of dealing with difficulties as opposed to blundering through.
7. Look for those who know that school improvement will require extra energy and that change will require skills they do not necessarily have but can learn.

Runkel et al. base their observations on many years of fieldwork, consulting, and research in school change.

In no place do Runkel et al. (1978), or I, require that the members of these task forces be representative. If the change agent in appointing this important body insists on equal representatives from grade levels, age, sex, subject matter, experience, and so on, the task force won't be a force. At best, it will be a representative discussion group. If you want action, select action people. If you want representation, devise other ways to supplement the task force with representative groups. This might include ex officio members, a recommendation review committee, or a faculty senate. The task force itself must be a small work group of fewer than 10 people.

The same concept of a work group of capable people versus representative groups applies at the building level. The principal should appoint or possibly have elected (after a careful discussion of the qualifications) the same kind of task force.

6.4 Time and Money

When reviewing strategies for change, two important considerations interact. They are time and money. A brief discussion is in order here.

Time is nature's way of assuring that everything does not happen all at once. Time is the change agent's friend. Time has been discussed earlier as a factor in student learning and it is certainly a large factor in adult learning as well. As has been stated, professional educators have been "taught" to think and act in certain ways—that are centralized, standardized, and homogenized. This means that the change process, in Kurt Lewin's terms, is a thawing out and refreezing process. Old ways must be "unlearned" and new ways assimilated. This mental and attitudinal process takes a lot of time. The time factor can be thought of in two ways. One is in terms of the mental maturation time for relearning, and the other concerns the very practical problem of arranging time for professional development activities.

The time it will take for the majority of teachers to accept their new roles and for the majority of administrators to modify their roles is difficult to predict. Again, look at the change matrix and judge how far a particular district has to go. In my experience as a consultant and from researching the general literature on change in schools, however, I would estimate about three years to go from a traditional, centralized system to a decentralized, empowered system. This time estimate assumes the board and top echelon are pushing this project, that there is careful planning, and that the change process is managed well. I talked with a superintendent who had decentralized his district, and he said it took ten years.

Now where do we get the time to conduct training sessions for the new order when we are so busy keeping our heads above water running the current system? Some compromises must be made. It's probable that, during the two- to three-year period of transition, the original system will be neglected and not as efficient as it might have been previously. If the leading administrators insist on peak efficiency as always during this time period, the new system will not happen. Set priorities about what *has* to be done, take a lean and mean attitude about essential administrative procedures, and invent expedient measures.

During this time period, all staff development monies and time must be allocated to the change process. No, districts cannot have a half-day for a book salesperson to speak to the teachers, nor can there be a discussion about a new reading series or time to worry about standardizing the discipline in the district. All adult learning, staff development, and professional advancement time must be devoted to the process of restructuring. This focus will last two to three years and then things can swing back to normal. Discussions and training regarding restructuring may be the last time that the district will come together for common training activities because leadership will handle this in the future. How serious are the decision makers about restructuring?

Let's talk money. It is possible to restructure without any increase in district funds. There will be some shifting of funds and line items and new priorities set, but the results of restructuring are not a matter of money. Restructuring is a matter of philosophy. There are, however, some budget considerations. The following is some advice:

- Be sure the director of budgets is completely informed and involved in the change process.
- Allocate all staff development monies to the change process for two to three years.
- Do not add any new administrators to the central office during this time period. If positions become vacant, replace them with "acting" personnel or merge the duties into those of another post.
- Do not make new large purchases of instructional materials for the district. "Save" this kind of money to be distributed among the school buildings as soon as each school is ready.
- Be prudent about substitute money as this can sometimes be used to free teachers for planning time.
- Do scan the government and foundations for possible grants and various external funding that will dovetail with restructuring.
- Do conduct budget training sessions for all principals and see that they are financially bonded if not now.
- Begin using principals in the budget planning process.
- Consider reducing travel costs for a short period of time.

Salary monies don't change; maintenance budgets will be the same during the transition; and general operations should not vary significantly. Consequently, do not let money arguments get in the way of restructuring. The total revenues available do not have to increase. As a matter of fact, some districts have approached restructuring as a means to save money by eliminating district office positions. This is not a sound reason for restructuring, and role shifts are all that are necessary in the district office. Greenholgh's *School Site Budgeting: Decentralized School Management* (1984) and Monk and Underwood's *Microlevel School Finance* (1988) are two books that will aid the change in the budget process.

6.5 A Change Model

A possible change model for the conversion might look as follows:

First Year

- Hold initial discussions regarding general feasibility among the administrative council.
- Involve principals in the concept with discussion, readings, trips to other districts, and general information gathering.
- Plan an administrative retreat or workshop for two days using an external consultant to lay the groundwork and review research and models.
- On at least one of these days, or at a separate time, hold a meeting that involves representatives of the school board, parents, and teachers.
- If the district has a teachers' union, it must be involved in the first year.
- Assess the needs of administrators related to the projected changes.
- Translate the training needs of administrators to a staff development plan. Specifically, principals will probably need training in participatory forms of governing such as the use of quality circles.
- Using a task force as described earlier, plan the implementation strategies for the next two to three years, including a time line in greater detail and anticipated staff development monies.

Second Year

- Ask the task force to clarify goals and objectives.
- Conduct the training sessions with administrators. Conduct building-level training sessions with teachers and building administrators.
- Plan the transition of designated management functions such as budget, personnel, curriculum, instruction, staff development, maintenance, transportation, and lunch services. These planning sessions should clarify the extent to which the system is to be restructured.
- Principals submit their plans to initiate building-level participatory management and, with approval, install the new system.
- Address the needs of the community with public information services at school board meetings, through district and school newsletters, and perhaps through public forums.
- Pay special attention to parents and provide them with information regarding the differences in programming in a decentralized system.
- Start some form of early transition by designating a pilot school or by designating staff development, textbook orders, and so on as means of practicing the new system. Staff development monies are a good place to start. Then perhaps work on curriculum and instruction functions while the centralized system is still intact.
- Have staff development training for support personnel.

Third Year

- Implement actual practices that decentralize management either with all of the schools or with those schools that have proven their readiness for autonomy. The degree of implementation needs to be determined during the second year.
- Report progress, problem areas, trouble spots, and so on to the board, the public, and parents. Be open about difficulties.
- Conduct evaluation activities as developed during the second year. Report, analyze, diagnose, and prescribe changes, alternatives, and options.

- Continue the decentralized management system making corrections and modifications based on data collected as agreed upon through the evaluation/feedback process.

Finally, there are some general questions for future planning, which will be conducted for the most part by individual building administrators:

- How can the budget be allocated more effectively?
- How effective are we in approaching the attainment of goals and objectives?
- How well is the program working in terms of increasing student achievement?
- How is the faculty helping to improve the instructional program?
- How well do the students feel the program is working for them?
- What unintended successes have occurred and what are the reasons?
- How well does the total school environment support program improvement?
- How do we "sell" the schools to the public?

Review of Key Concepts

❑ A definition of educational leadership in restructured systems must include the leader as a change agent.

❑ The key components of the change process are readiness to change, careful planning, monitoring the implementation, and evaluating the process.

❑ Successful organizational change requires high-involvement management.

❑ Selecting a leadership task force is a crucial step in restructuring.

❑ A total restructuring of a traditional school district will take at least three years.

❑ Restructuring may not cost more money, but it will require shifts in financial priorities.

References

Greenholgh, J. (1984). *School site budgeting: Decentralized school management.* New York: University Press of America.

Hersey, P., & Blanchard, K. (1988). *Management of organizational behavior.* Englewood Cliffs, NJ: Prentice-Hall.

Monk, D., & Underwood, J. (Eds.). (1988). *Microlevel school finance.* Cambridge, MA: Bollinger (for the American Education Finance Association).

Runkel, P., Schmuck, R., Arends, J., & Francis, R. (1978). *Transforming the school's capacity for problem solving.* Eugene: University of Oregon, Center for Educational Policy and Management.

7

How to Maintain Accountability During and After Restructuring

How can one not believe in accountability? Yet educators, through sins of omission, created a void. This void is found in the educational sequence of *pay taxes = educate the youth of our state = show evidence of educator productivity* (input-throughput-output). The political question is simple: "Are we getting our monies' worth?" For too long, public educators, living in the comfort of a monopoly, failed to develop plausible systems of accountability. I am *not* asserting that educators of the past did not do a good job given the resources of their time, but I am submitting that public school educators failed to demonstrate progress in ways understood by the public and legislators.

State legislators, taxpayers, departments of public instruction, university authorities, commercial test companies, and parts of the private sector have assumed responsibility for accountability. The above are unquestionably important stakeholders in the public schools, but basic professional accountability should be the responsibility of the profession—any profession.

When talking with my chiropractor recently, he informed me that, as a member of the professional ethics committee of his state chiropractic association, he was traveling to another city to aid in the investigation of a malpractice complaint. The committee has the responsibility for making a recommendation to the state licensing board, which may eventually affect the professional future of the doctor in question. There probably are some flaws in this system, but can you imagine a teacher in a public school being asked to serve on a comparable education committee? Why not? How can educators at all levels take charge of accountability within their own ranks and within their own organizations? In the empowered school of the future, this will be one of the responsibilities.

7.1 What Are the Board of Education's Imperatives?

The local board of education is the traditional governing body of public schools. While boards must adhere to federal and state guidelines, laws, and policies, they still have a significant impact on the operations of each school. In fact, local board members and the superintendent may be able to affect the state governing bodies through lobbying and political influence. Because each state is different in its approach and in its policies, this chapter will concentrate on the local board and local administrators.

Consequently, a cogent question is this: "What does the board of education want?" Because board members are typically lay people, they need some expert opinions from professional educators as they make decisions. Of course, collaboration among board members, the superintendent, and the professional staff is not always a positive experience. School systems need to strive toward excellence, however, regardless of local squabbles and school board-administrator differences. The school system cannot progress (although it can survive) without direction from the local school board.

This is where long-range, strategic planning becomes important. Accountability at the local level can be established only if there are stated goals and expectations in the first place. Based on the superintendent's recommendations, the board should establish and publicize their long-range goals and their annual objectives each year. The categories of these goal statements can be academic, philosophical, financial, or/and pedagogical. The details of this kind of specific leadership have been covered in other volumes, such as in Roger Kaufman's *Planning Educational Systems* (1988) and *Mapping Educational Success* (1992), James Lewis, Jr.'s *Long Range and Short Range Planning for Educational Administrators* (1983), Roger Carlson and Gary Awkerman's *Educational Planning* (1991), and George Odiorne's *MBO II* (1979).

A study of specific techniques and a decision-making process that is positive and productive will place the direction *for* the system *from* its leadership. What are the board imperatives? What has to be accomplished? What should be accomplished? Once the imperatives are known, the district can develop means by which to measure the efforts of the system and the staff. For example, if the board, upon recommendation from the superintendent and staff, decide that it is imperative that all students become computer literate before they graduate, then budgets, staff development, curriculum, and instruction all are affected. But perhaps most of all, the accountability issues are affected. The district is accountable for whether in fact students are computer literate, depending on the percentage of mastery previously agreed upon.

7.2 Using the Good Side of MBO

One system of managing organizations that has been available for several decades is referred to as management by objectives (MBO). While MBO systems have been criticized mildly in some of the literature, MBO remains one of the most effective ways to manage restructured school districts. MBOs can assist in the transition period of restructuring as well as in the daily operations once restructuring has been implemented.

The system is quite simple and will work if everyone understands the procedures and if the process has definite administrative support. One variation could follow the sequence below:

(1) The school board, with guidance from the superintendent, establishes long-range goals to be accomplished in a three- to five-year time period. Teacher representatives can have input to this process if the board is comfortable with this.

Example A. *Goal:* To increase the writing skills of all students, a long-range plan to institute "writing across the curriculum" will be established. *Objective:* Within a one-year time period, each school building will develop a proposal that establishes their plan for implementing a "writing across the curriculum" instructional strategy.

Example B. *Goal:* Within a five-year time frame, the school district governance will be decentralized under a school site management plan. *Objective:* Each school building, using teacher participation, will develop a proposal for their acceptance as a site-managed school, which will include an evaluation plan. Progress reports on the five-year goal will be filed each year.

(2) At least in part, district office administrators' performance reviews will be based on the annual objectives they set that are related to the district goals and objectives.

(3) Each *school building administrator* sets long-range goals and short-range objectives that detail how the district goals and objectives will be accomplished. Teacher input, using one of the plans discussed earlier, is an essential part of this process—but procedures can differ in each building. Additional goals and objectives not related to the district goals may be set by any building. These plans should be approved by some district-level authority. A word of caution regarding this approval process: If

the scrutiny is too precise, the empowerment tone can be minimized to the point of being ineffective.

Example. *Goal:* This school will develop curriculum and instructional strategies that incorporate writing skills in every subject and grade level. *Objective:* In the first year of implementation, the English department will conduct one in-service day for the faculty regarding appropriate writing skills that can be taught and integrated into the various disciplines.

(4) Within each school building, depending on the internal organization, smaller units such as teams or departments will establish their unit goals and objectives, which match school-level goals and objectives.

(5) Each professional school-level employee sets annual objectives that are in part based on the school's goals and objectives.

(6) Each small group, team, or department establishes goals and objectives that relate to the school's goals and objectives.

Example A. *Goal:* (middle school math team): The unit will emphasize the writing aspects of the math curriculum over the next five years and evaluate every year. *Objective:* In the next year, teachers will integrate a 10% increase in story problems and request that students write (construct) at least one story problem per week.

Example B. *Goal:* The middle school math team will install a quality circle process as their decision-making model for their unit. *Objective:* At the end of one year, an evaluation will be made of the quality circle process used within the unit to determine whether that mode is productive, and a second-year process will be determined based on that initial evaluation.

(7) Annual unit and employee performance reviews will reveal the relative success of the overall MBO system and the particular goal achievements and, based on that information, continue to revise and set new goals and objectives for the next time period.

Example. The goal of integrating writing skills across the curriculum has received mixed reviews on its success. The board determines that it is still a worthwhile goal and requests the process continue for another two years for a new evaluation concerning future processes.

The goal of implementing school site management has been accomplished successfully and is considered to be internalized in the system. A few small units are still undecided about their decision-making process and will continue to work on that objective for another year. New governance process long-range goals may be devised for the next five-year cycle, but, at this juncture, the goal has been accomplished.

Thus an integration of system and unit goals and employee goals related to those system goals has been accomplished. The MBO actually moves the system along, always interjecting new ideas, innovations, and school and program improvement. Teachers are empowered, participative management has been practiced, and restructuring has manifested school improvement results.

In regard to goal setting, Bailey (1991) states:

> This is high risk management. If you do not set goals, you will not have to meet them. If you set them and keep them hidden, people will forget they exist. If you don't set them [goals] you will be left complaining more about the importance of standardized testing because someone is going to fill the accountability void. (p. 140)

Bailey (1991) also lists some example areas on which goals could be based:

(a) standardized achievement scores;
(b) across the curriculum or core areas such as writing, thinking, problem solving;
(c) student behavior;
(d) student attendance;
(e) school-constructed achievement tests;
(f) retention of specific course material and knowledge;

(g) special program progress such as music, special education, and so on;

(h) success of human relations programs;

(i) experimental programs such as programs without grade levels;

(j) teacher and student attitudes about scheduling;

(k) involvement levels of after-school activities;

(l) evaluation of faculty development programs;

(m) parental involvement activities;

(n) public relation activities;

(o) counseling programs, in terms of numbers and quality; and

(p) individual school's accomplishment of district goals. (p. 141)

7.3 During Restructuring

During the transition period of restructuring, there are several methods of collecting data. They are data survey feedback, organizational and job analysis, role mapping, and curriculum mapping. There are adequate technologies available for each of these methods and they will be described briefly.

A. The Craft of Data Survey Feedback

There is a rapidly growing body of professionals who are learning and teaching the craft of data survey feedback that is applicable in terms of accountability. Action research, program evaluation, organizational development, and management information systems all depend upon accurate data collected in the form of questionnaires, surveys, or opinionnaires. The basic procedures to follow to devise an instrument for these purposes follows (remember that this kind of data collecting process is directed toward identifying needs and problems and providing information that will facilitate decision making):

- Establish a theory base that relates to the topic.
- Write in an open-ended form first to allow expression of topic ideas.

- Modify and write a draft "objective" form (questions, opinions, and so on).
- Review, edit, and pilot test for readability.
- Write the final form with a scaling (rating) format.
- Administer the instrument (usually anonymously).
- Analyze and record results.
- Develop action plans for solutions or change.
- Usually, readminister the same form periodically to note changes.

Example. The superintendent knows that staff readiness is an important change ingredient. She wants to convert the system to school site management (*theory base*). A draft of a questionnaire to determine staff readiness starts with the *open-ended* question, "Are we ready?" From this beginning, a *draft objective form* is prepared; for example, "What is your readiness state for school site management?" The question is *edited* for readability. The *scaling* format is added, "On a scale of 1 to 5, with 5 representing extreme readiness, what is your readiness for school site management?" This question and others are *administered* to the administrative staff. The results are *analyzed* (the average response is 4.1). *Action planning* is implemented based on the favorable report. *Follow-up* could include checking on the comfort level a year after installation.

The follow-up process and/or decisions based on the data are very important. The process generally is best done in a "public" fashion. Faculty and staff normally should be informed of the result. This "going public" (within the organization) can be done three basic ways:

Waterfall. With the waterfall method, every layer of the organization sees the same results but in sequential time periods. For example, the board of education would see the report and pass it on to the central office and then to the buildings.

Top-down. The top-down method follows the sequence of the waterfall but editing may take place at any level. There may be some proper reasons that teachers do not get specific information from the data that the board receives. Proper reasons might include that (a) the topic is of no interest to the next group, (b) there are ethical or confidential reasons for withholding information, or (c) there is concern that the data are not valid or reliable. Officials would be wise to be very prudent in their use of the top-down method of disseminating.

Simultaneously. This method is the best for an empowered system because it is more open and everyone receives the information at the same time. This minimizes rumors. The dissemination can occur at a large meeting or through simultaneous mailings.

Two good references for data survey procedures are D. G. Bowers and J. L. Franklin's *Data-Based Organizational Change* (1977) and J. L. Bowditch and A. F. Buono's *Quality of Worklife Assessment* (1982).

B. *Organizational and Job Analysis*

Corporate business executives and consultants to corporations have established ways to analyze personnel functions and organizational effectiveness. The literature is replete with instruments, procedures, and designs to determine effectiveness. Particular attention has been paid to control and power, which will be emphasized in this section. Empowerment as a result of restructuring is crucial to organizational effectiveness; however, typical educational organizations have not placed emphasis on the analytical aspects of a balance of power. School systems have assumed that there were district office personnel, building administrators, and teachers. But what do all of these people really do, and where is the power located? Yes, most districts today have a table of organization, and they may have job descriptions, but these positions are seldom analyzed or modified.

Consequently, part of the accountability scramble is to determine what all employees are doing, who has power, who is supposed to have power, and what modifications are in order. There are consultant firms that provide sophisticated designs, but a simple procedure is used here as an example of the kind of diagnosis and analysis that is possible to accomplish using internal consultants. This basic concept is adapted from Practical Management, Inc.'s booklet, *Organization Diagnosis* (1980).

Construct a worksheet matrix with the personnel given administrative decision-making responsibilities listed vertically. Remember, in a restructured system, teachers, teacher work groups, quality circles as well as designated administrators should be included. On the horizontal of the matrix, list all major functions requiring decisions. An example is shown Figure 7.1.

Code. In each cell in the matrix, score the current functioning with the following code:

9 = makes final decision
8 = recommends final decision
7 = makes tentative decision that is usually approved ("rubber stamp")
6 = makes recommendation for a decision that needs approval
5 = is asked for opinion and input as an individual
4 = is part of a small decision-making group (e.g., consensus)
3 = has a vote within the large group (faculty meeting)
2 = is encouraged to make requests, submit ideas, propose (influence)
1 = has no power in this regard

Directions. Total both the personnel columns and the decision function columns. Compare the totals assigned to each position and determine whether there is "underpower" or "overpower" for the new structure. What is the ideal, without consideration of personalities? What about the functions? Are too many people involved in a particular function? Is there "overinput" or "underinput" in terms of this function? In a restructured system, it will be very important to determine the correct balance. The degrees of participation are analyzed, diagnosed, and modified. This accountability matrix can be disseminated to stakeholders or at least the board of education so there is an understanding of who is doing what and what group needs to do more or perform better.

This can all be done in a climate of collegiality. It should not be a "witch hunt," but the reality of organizational effectiveness

Personnel	Decision Function					
	Budget	*Merit increases*	*Hiring*	*Textbook*	*Selection*	*Training*
Superintendent						
Assistant Superintendent						
Administration's council						
Principals						
Principal's council						
Work teams						
Quality circles						
Classroom teacher						

Figure 7.1. School System Diagnosis Matrix

and the players' roles is a part of accountability not often considered. This diagnosis can also have implications for salary disbursements. Are you paying the right people their fair share? Are there specific teachers who are serving on many committees and are there teachers who are not serving at all? The matrix can be applied districtwide or it can be modified to apply to an individual building or subunit. Being accountable also includes asserting a reasonable balance of salaries spent on personnel as well as their respective power and influence.

Examples of resources in addition to *Organization Diagnosis* are T. S. Bateman and G. R. Ferris's *Methods and Analysis in Organizational Research* (1984) and Marvin Weisbord's *Organizational Diagnosis: A Workbook of Theory and Practice* (1978).

c. Role Mapping

Role mapping is an accountability device that enables decision makers to determine more accurately how the organization works. Analyzing the organization using role mapping is a specific process that is designed to improve functioning in a way that might not be uncovered in a simple job analysis. Job analysis tends to show what is supposed to be happening, but role mapping gets at reality. Role mapping is a graphic representation of how an organization works. The following components can be "mapped": relationships, process flow (e.g., purchase orders), role matrix (as seen in job analysis), performance support systems or support people, and knowledge (information) sources.

The concept was originally designed to show the flow of raw materials to the organization, the production of goods, and the service necessary to market the goods. Role mapping illustrates each employee's part in the final outcome of marketing the product or, in the case of schools, the service. Graphic representations will aid understanding the importance of each role (see Figures 7.2, 7.3, and 7.4). Tables 7.1, 7.2, and 7.3 are meant to be self-explanatory. Used as diagnostic tools, they will allow you to carefully discern your organization's functioning.

More details can be found in the following sources: T. F. Gilbert's *Human Competence* (1978), R. I. James's *The No Nonsense Guide*

TABLE 7.1 Management Functions

1. Management starts with the market.
     Who are the customers / parents?

2. Establish measurement criteria and standards for quality
     (accountability).
     What are the customer's requirements for our services?

3. Adjust standards established by the market.
     How do our services compare with those of other schools?

4. Establish ongoing program evaluation.
     What is our quality review process?

5. Hire and develop faculty.
     What is the level of performance and what are our expectations?

6. Organize people and functions effectively.
     What is the best structure to meet the needs?

7. Establish the curriculum.
     What does the market want?
     What do the stakeholders want?
     What are the key roles?

8. Procure materials, equipment, and supplies.
     Do we have the proper technology?

9. Secure resources and support services.
     What are the available options?

---

to *Common Sense Management* (1989), or G. A. Rummler's *Introduction to Performance Technology: Organizations as Systems* (1986).

D. *Curriculum Mapping*

Curriculum mapping is the brain child of Fenwick English (see English, 1980, 1992), now the head of the Department of Educational Administration at the University of Cincinnati. In the same spirit of role mapping as a management improvement process, curriculum mapping gets at what is actually being taught on a day-to-day basis. English (1980, p. 558) states, "Many school districts appear not to have grasped the rather

TABLE 7.2 Analyzing Roles

1. Look for performer accomplishments.
2. Do not indict a specific performer.
3. Where are the problems?
4. Are problems due to
   expectations?
   job descriptions?
   structural breakdown?
   relationships?
   process flow?
5. Talk to people about their jobs in a realistic way.
6. Is comprehension of the role an issue?
7. Link each job to the organization and its market.
8. Expectations:

Principal's *expectations*	*Teacher's own* *expectations*
1.	1.
2.	2.
3.	3.
4.	4.
5.	5.

TABLE 7.3 Knowledge

* What is necessary technology?
* Where is resource information?
* What are the policy guidelines?
* Who can help you?
* Where are questions answered?
* Where are decisions made?
* What is the subject matter?
* What are key references?
* How important is this knowledge?

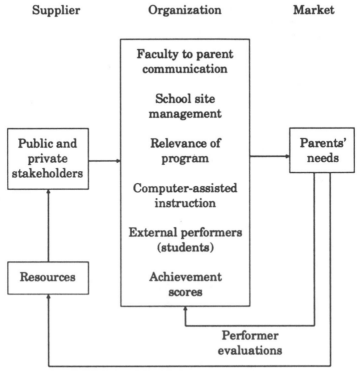

Figure 7.2. A Role Relationship Map
NOTE: Each function of management must have a clear view of its relationship to the customer (parent). How does the organization relate to its customers?

fundamental fact of life that 'the guide ain't the curriculum.' " There is room for flexibility in application, but the typical maps contain the actual content taught in each subject and the time spent on each topic. The subject matter taught can be divided into concepts, skills, and attitudes, and the corresponding time spent on each is reported. Curriculum mapping tells a staff or a principal or a supervisor what is actually being taught, how long it is being taught, and how consistent teachers are within the same subject. It provides a discrepancy view of what is supposed to be taught (the curriculum guide) and what is actually being

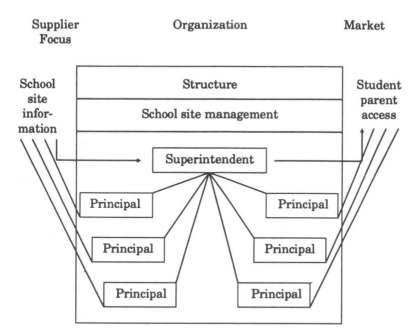

Figure 7.3. Organizational Structure Relationship Map
NOTE: School site management increases access levels and changes roles. Every performer is connected to another performer and/or the market (parents). What goes on between the boxes (internal), and what goes on between the boxes and the market (external)?

taught. English stresses that by mapping we can come closer to congruence in the real curriculum and the written curriculum.

As in other maps, some sort of graphic should be developed. The graphic not only summarizes the content and time but displays the "big picture" for easy viewing. A simple table or a matrix for each subject can provide the visual effect desired. Teams of teachers should do their own map, which would be much more effective than a supervisor creating maps for them. While I am discussing curricular mapping in the "During Restructuring" section, it can be used periodically after restructuring to give quick readouts as to what is actually being taught. Let's look at some devices that might be used after restructuring to provide a thorough accountability system.

A Site-Based High School

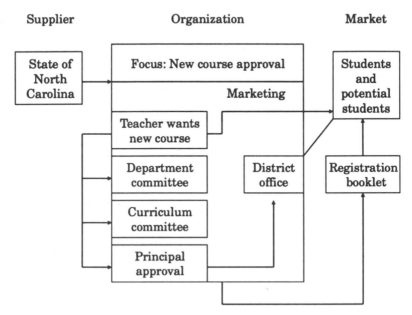

Figure 7.4. Process Flow Map
NOTE: A process flow describes the sequence of accomplishments required to produce a specific service or a desired output. In analyzing, you should trace *real* accomplishments—not what you are doing (e.g., finished typing report versus "typing").

7.4 After Restructuring

A. *Curriculum Auditing*

After restructuring has been chosen and is being implemented, there is a continued need to demonstrate accountability to parents and taxpayers. Again, we can sit still and accept the legislated versions of accountability, usually in the form of state standardized testing, or we can be proactive and account for ourselves. Because curriculum and learning are our business, it makes sense to thoroughly understand what and why we are teaching.

One management tool recommended by Fenwick English (1988) is called "curriculum auditing" (compared with curriculum mapping, an audit is more thorough, takes longer, and involves larger issues such as school climate). While curriculum auditing should be happening periodically in any school district, it is crucial in a restructured school. Some of the traditional forms of accountability have been changed. These might have included state curriculum guidelines, district curriculum policy, and past practice. A thorough audit of the curriculum on repeated occasions is the best way to assure curricular accountability.

"A curricular audit is a process of examining documents and practices that exist within a peculiar institution normally called a school in a given time, culture, and society" (English, 1988, p. 33). There is a technology involved in an audit, it assesses quantity and quality, and it provides a description of the extent to which the actual meets the ideal. Perhaps the most important aspect of a curricular audit is that it forces school people to think about their ideal. But the quote from English is particularly germane to schools in the process of improving through restructuring. Change is cultural, and an audit must be viewed in the cultural setting in which it occurs—time, local culture, and the society at large.

The standards of an audit, which stem from some basic assumptions, form the framework through which data can be gathered. Those basic assumptions are as follows:

- The school district is able to demonstrate its control of resources, programs, and personnel.
- The school district has established clear and valid objectives for students.
- The school district has documentation explaining how its programs have been developed, implemented, and conducted.
- The school district uses results from the district-designed or adopted assessments to adjust, improve, or terminate ineffective practices.
- The school district has been able to improve productivity.

The data are collected using these five standards and the methodology used can be data survey instruments, interviews, documentation searches, or observations (including photography). The audit can be done by an outside consultant who might spend a week in an average district or, with training, internal consultants can serve as well. I have trained graduate students, in a semester, to do limited audits in districts, and they have performed very well. There is a technology to be learned but the big issue is that districts need to look at themselves—particularly after restructuring, when they cannot rely on state guidelines.

The single best resource is Fenwick English's *Curriculum Auditing* (1988).

B. *Using Outcome Indicators*

How do the faculty of an empowered, restructured school know whether their instructional delivery system is effective? They can rely on test scores as established by the state or they can develop local demonstrations of accountability. One system advocated in the literature is referred to as "outcome indicators."

Outcome indicators can be applied at the state, district, or local levels. The preference of the faculty at a site-based school would be the school building level. "Local indicators of success," as they are sometimes referred to, need not countermand state or district standards or expectations. The advantage of indicators applied at the local school is that parents and faculty can agree on the expected learning and behavioral outcomes that are unique to their school. This personalizes the accountability process.

As an example, Rathbone (1988) conducted a study in Delaware and reported an examination of a process model to determine an individual school's success depending on the outcome objectives established by the faculty. Results of the study demonstrated that various subgroups at local high schools can arrive at a consensus regarding important indicator choices and that the process was instrumental in raising awareness regarding the school's goals and objectives and in planning for school improvement.

The actual indicators can be stated in qualitative or quantitative terms. They can deal with achievement, attendance, discipline, extracurricular activities, homework, or whatever is considered important by the building staff. This process also is a wonderful opportunity to involve parents and leading citizens in school improvement and accountability. The list of indicators may be rather extensive (i.e., 20 to 30) or they might be confined to several major statements. Rathbone makes the point that no one indicator, such as an achievement score, can be used to measure school success. Consequently, multiple indicators as determined at the local site come much closer to explaining the complex social phenomenon of schooling. The basic question school personnel must ask is this: "Are we serving our community?" Judging a school on this basic criterion can be accomplished by the use of outcome indicators. It is fairly simple; given a specified time line, the school has either accomplished an indicator or they have not. What is your school's score?

The point of this chapter is to illustrate alternatives and supplements to standardized testing. Technology, references, and models have been provided. A superintendent of a system of schools, then, needs to allow individual schools to select from district-approved systems or combinations of systems. Principals, involving their staff, need to select from the alternatives and implement, evaluate, and modify. Someone needs to report the results of the accountability measures to the public, to the press, and, of course, to the school board.

Please do not let the excuse of the lack of accountability measures prevent your school system from moving forward. Real school leaders choose the ways in which they are going to be held accountable!

Review of Key Concepts

❏ The ongoing question regarding accountability is this: What does the school board want?

❏ Managing by objectives (MBO) is a positive management practice that can be used before, during, and after restructuring.

❏ Evidence of accountability must come from a variety of sources, and standardized testing must be viewed as only one of those sources.

❑ Certain technologies now available to us will assist in delivering an accountability picture. They include data survey feedback, job analysis, role mapping, curriculum mapping, curriculum auditing, and the use of outcome indicators.

References

Bailey, W. J. (1991). *School-site management applied.* Lancaster, PA: Technomic.

Bateman, T. S., & Ferris, G. R. (1984). *Methods and analysis in organizational research.* Reston, VA: Reston.

Bowditch, J. L., & Buono, A. F. (1982). *Quality of worklife assessment.* Boston: Auburn House.

Bowers, D. G., & Franklin, J. L. (1977). *Data-based organizational change.* La Jolla, CA: University Associates.

Carlson, R., & Awkerman, G. (Eds.). (1991). *Educational planning.* New York: Longman.

English, F. (1980, April). Curriculum mapping. *Educational Leadership,* 558-559.

English, F. (1988). *Curriculum auditing.* Lancaster, PA: Technomic.

English, F. (1992). *Deciding what to teach and test: Developing, aligning, and auditing the curriculum.* Newbury Park, CA: Corwin.

Gilbert, T. F. (1978). *Human competence.* New York: McGraw-Hill.

James, R. I. (1989). *The no nonsense guide to common sense management.* (Available from James Associates, 9260 Orangedale Ave., Orangedale, CA 95662)

Kaufman, R. (1988). *Planning educational systems.* Lancaster, PA: Technomic.

Kaufman, R. (1992). *Mapping educational success: Strategic thinking and planning for school administrators.* Newbury Park, CA: Corwin.

Lewis, J., Jr. (1983). *Long range and short range planning for educational administrators.* Boston: Allyn & Bacon.

Odiorne, G. (1979). *MBO II.* Belmont, CA: Fearon Pitman.

Practical Management, Inc. (1980). *Organization diagnosis.* Calabasas, CA: Practical Management.

Rathbone, S. (1988). *A process model for the determination of indicators of school success* (Executive Position Paper). Newark: University of Delaware.

Rummler, G. A. (1986). *Introduction to performance technology: Organizations as systems.* Washington, DC: NSPI Publications.

Weisbord, M. (1978). *Organizational diagnosis: A workbook of theory and practice.* Reading, MA: Addison-Wesley.

Troubleshooting Guide

NOTES

NOTES

NOTES

NOTES

NOTES

NOTES

NOTES

NOTES

NOTES